FOUNDING AND FUNDING FAMILY LITERACY PROGRAMS

A How-To-Do-It Manual for Librarians

Carole Talan

**HOW-TO-DO-IT MANUALS
FOR LIBRARIANS**

NUMBER 92

NEAL-SCHUMAN PUBLISHERS, INC.
New York, London

Published by Neal-Schuman Publishers, Inc.
100 Varick Street
New York, NY 10013

Printed and bound in the United States of America.

Library of Congress Cataloging-in-Publication Data

    Founding and funding family literacy programs : a how-to-do-it
manual / Carole Talan.
      p.   cm. — (How-do-do-it manuals for librarians : no. 92)
    Includes bibliographical references and index.
    ISBN 1-55570-210-4
    1. Libraries and new literates—United States.   2. Family literacy
programs—United States.   3. Public libraries—Services to
illiterate persons—United States. I. Title. II. Series: How-to-
do-it manuals for libraries ; no. 92.
Z716.45.T35 1999
027.6—dc21   98-54790
                                                          CIP

CONTENTS

Appendices

PREFACE

Family literacy programs are now recognized as the most effective solution to the age-old program of illiteracy. They work because they combine fundamental educational practices that foster the development of literacy and preliteracy skills with sound parenting practices (such as modeling positive reading behavior in the home and stimulating language development from birth). Fostering family literacy is not a new role for libraries. For decades, libraries have provided many of the components of family literacy: programs on parenting and child development, lapsits, read-alouds, storytimes, and a variety of other programming.

Although libraries do offer a wide variety of these programs to support family literacy, most place the library and the librarian in a supportive role, supplying programs that help meet the goals of other community groups. *Founding and Funding Family Literacy Programs* takes a totally different approach because it shows how the library and its staff can be positioned as the leader in such efforts. Following the ideas outlined here, the library becomes not just a provider of some of the program components— or one of many partners in the total family literacy program—but rather the community's *primary* family literacy provider. Libraries are perfectly positioned to play this role because they are almost always the most logical, resource-filled, and accessible service agency in a given community.

Founding and Funding Family Literacy Programs is primarily directed at adult services and/or children's librarians who are working to position the library as their community's primary family literacy agency. Nevertheless, family literacy also clearly affects other departments in the library. It would serve the community well if the director, other librarians, and the trustees were familiar with the concepts and programs described here. Because *Founding and Funding Family Literacy Programs* covers not only the steps in developing a library-based family literacy program, but also the all-important question of funding, this is also a book to share with the Friends group and with other community organizations that might play a role in the library's family literacy program.

The book's organization assumes no previous experience with family literacy programs. Chapter 1, "What is Family Literacy?" defines the term, provides historical perspective, and explains the need for such programs.

Chapter 2, "Who Is Offering Programs?" describes several well-established, successful family-literacy programs, showing what is possible and what has worked. This chapter offers material for sparking the interest of potential funders.

Chapter 3, "Could You Bring a Family Program to Your Library?" how starting a library-based family literacy program benefits both the community and the library.

Chapter 4, "What Does Your Community Need?" deals with assessing the needs and resources of the community and includes copy-ready survey forms.

Chapter 5, "How Do You Start?" covers development of the actual program. Step-by-step instructions for creating programs are augmented by tips on addressing the four basic components of family literacy and two model programs.

Chapter 6, "Who Pays for the Program?" describes how the program can bring money into the library, the principles of successful partnerships, and ways that serving special populations can attract funding and partnerships to the library.

Chapter 7, "Will Anyone Show Up?" presents ideas for recruitment and retention of families, tips for training family literacy tutors, advice on developing a manual for tutors, and suggested ways of reaching families who cannot attend regularly scheduled events.

Chapter 8, "Children's Books for the Whole Family," discusses using children's books for family literacy, helping families build their own home libraries, reading aloud, and discussing parenting with participants in the program. Because there are so many parents who themselves need to develop reading skills, the chapter also explains why children's books are good for adults, particularly new adult readers, and what the important qualities of children's books for new adult readers are.

Chapter 9, "Following Up with Evaluation," provides guidelines for evaluation.

Chapter 10, "How Can Libraries *Not* Be Involved?" is a brief afterword responding to this crucial question.

Nine appendices provide materials to help libraries get started or quickly expand existing programs: sample lessons from two programs that provide family literacy training; a bibliography of easy-to-read parenting books; a sample memorandum of agreement between the library and another organization, in this case the local Head Start program; a list of pointers for new adult readers on how to help their children develop a love of reading; a sample agenda for training tutors; sample materials for tutor manuals; a bibliography of appropriate children's books for family literacy; and a family literacy survey to use with parents.

Librarians or other interested community members who read *Founding and Funding Family Literacy Programs* will understand why it makes such good sense to entrust the role of primary provider to the library. The reader will also have a good grasp of the purpose and nature of family literacy and will know how to establish a program in the community's public library. If libraries in every community take the lead, they can make great strides toward eradicating illiteracy.

John Zickefoose, Corona Public Library, Families for Literacy Program

Photo by Carolyn Morse/Community Publication group. *Reprinted with Permission.*

ACKNOWLEDGMENTS

This publication is the result of many years of work and has benefitted from the input and support of a number of people in the field of family literacy.

This guide would not have been possible without the many Families for Literacy (FFL) staff at local public libraries throughout California. It is their work that has made the past ten years of my life an enriching, fulfilling adventure in family literacy. I am grateful for their support and their guidance and am ever in awe of the incredible work that they do. They achieve so much with so little and truly do "make a difference."

Thanks, too, to the many FFL families who shared their stories, their writings, and their photos with me. They are remarkable, brave, and dedicated people, who are making an effort to put their children and their families first in their lives.

I am especially indebted to Jane Curtis, Robin Levy, and Beth Bochser (all active or former FFL coordinators) for reviewing the original manuscript and making helpful suggestions and additions based on their own experiences working with library-based family literacy. Beth also kindly agreed to share many of her original materials, which have been so effective in her program. Thanks, too, to Penny Peck for reading the revised manuscript and offering her input from the viewpoint of a children's librarian; to Ruth Nickse and Ellen Goldsmith for their willingness to share their ideas and their knowledge; and to Susan Roman of theAssociation for Library Services to Children at the American Library Association for never letting me lose faith.

A special thanks to my fellow members of the remarkable Red Boa Society (Nora, Judy, Susan, Gray, and Beth) who have helped me through these ten years of family literacy challenges with their humor, insight, and love. We are such different people but united in our commitment to what we believe is the right of all people, to be literate and to raise literate children.

And, to my best friend, partner, companion, lover, and all around cheerleader, thanks for those many days, nights, and weekends spent patiently waiting for me to finish this manuscript and its revisions so we could regain our leisure time for skiing and boating. Without your support and love, Hans, this guide would never have been completed and, without you, my life wouldn't be complete. You make it all worthwhile! (and congratulations on your BIG day!)

January 16, 1999

1 WHAT IS FAMILY LITERACY?

My children are learning more every day. They like to go to the library. They like to work on their homework more now, now that they see my husband doing his homework too. They all sit around him so he can help them.

—Mom at Chula Vista (Calif.)
Public Library's family literacy program

FAMILY LITERACY DEFINED

Both "family" and "literacy" have been adequately defined in the dictionary. Defining family literacy, however, involves more than just combining these two definitions into one.

For most people the definition of family literacy depends upon the context in which they seek to define it. Definitions both abound and vary considerably—from brief statements that define family literacy as any model providing literacy activities within a family setting, to much longer and involved definitions in which all possible aspects are clearly defined and delineated.

For the purposes of this manual, a concise, abbreviated version of the definition as found in the Head Start Authorization Act of 1994 will be used. Once one has filtered through the government verbiage, the following basic components are found.

FAMILY LITERACY IN ITS FULL POTENTIAL PROVIDES:

a. Literacy improvement and enrichment for the adult, as needed.
b. Emerging literacy activities and opportunities for the child, with emphasis on, but not limited to, the preschool and primary child.
c. Interactive/intergenerational activities for the adult(s), and child(ren).
d. Parenting development and discussion opportunities.

HISTORICAL PERSPECTIVE

Family literacy is not the new kid on the block for libraries. From the minute libraries took on the cause of literacy in the early 1900s to the moment they began programming for children, public libraries have been immersed in the fundamental concepts of family literacy. After all, even before embarking on direct literacy instruction for adults, libraries were already part of the literacy scene. For most new immigrants and even native-born, nonliterate Americans, the public library was the one place where they could access the tools of literacy without cost. Even the poorest could afford that!

Libraries were the first adult basic education institutions in our country. Long before adult schools and community colleges were envisioned as public services, public libraries were holding classes and providing resources for both those in need of learning English as their second language (ESL) and for native speakers wanting to become literate or improve their basic literacy skills. It was partially the success of these early sessions in public libraries that eventually led to the beginning of adult education in the basic skills of reading, writing, and math.

Although the literacy needs of the adult are important, they comprise only one of the four elements of family literacy: literacy for the adult, emerging literacy for children, interactive/intergenerational literacy, and parenting. The second important component, the emerging literacy needs of the child, was also addressed early on by libraries. Attention to the development of collections of quality children's literature quickly became the mark of a good public library. Libraries soon found that provision of special programming for children, particularly preschool children, was a role that they filled well.

This is not to say that the adoption of this role for children in the public library was without controversy. In the early years, even children's services had its detractors in the library world, those who were not convinced that this was an appropriate service for public libraries. However, by time the children's division of the American Library Association (ALA) was formed in the early 1900s, the adoption of children's services and programming was on its way to becoming complete in many public libraries. It would become, for most public libraries, a regular service, just like adult services and reference.

Interactive and intergenerational activities for families are somewhat newer to public libraries. Many libraries that previously held special programming only for children, now invite the parents to participate also. Some libraries even plan and conduct family nights to encourage the active involvement of the entire family. Most of these changes have been brought about because of the realization by the public library that parents do not always value reading and books in the home or know how to instill a love and joy of books in their children. They often need to be shown why and how to read aloud to their children and to see modeling of effective techniques for reading aloud.

The last component of family literacy, parenting, is also not new to libraries. Libraries have long held excellent collections of books and manuals on parenting. What *is* new, however, is the more proactive

Family literacy is adults and children reading and loving books together.

stance that many public libraries have already taken in providing special expert guests and programming on parenting issues. This has been viewed by most as a natural means for addressing the needs expressed by their communities.

Both school and public libraries are considered essential elements to educating youth and adults. Public libraries have long been recognized as valuable contributors to the emerging literacy needs of preschool children. What has been missing, however, for many libraries, is that all-important, holistic connecting link among these services—focus on the family.

WHAT IS THE PROBLEM?

The problem in America is that the number of adults who lack adequate literacy skills has increased dramatically. The National Adult Literacy Survey (NALS) establishes four levels of literacy. Levels I and II are addressed here. According to *The State of Literacy in America* (1998:4)[1] the National Institute for Literacy's (NIFL) publication of Stephen Reder's Synthetic Estimates of Adult Literacy Proficiency based on NALS results, adults in Level I are those most urgently in need of literacy skills. These adults can usually sign their names, locate a single piece of information in a sports article, or find the expiration date on a driver's license. Most of these adults are not "illiterate," but they usually unable to perform more complex literacy tasks such as locating eligibility from a table of employee benefits or a street intersection on a map, or correctly entering background information on a social security card application. Forty-three percent of adults at this level live in poverty. Level II adults could do all the tasks above that Level I could not perform, but are generally unable to perform more intricate tasks using documents of greater length or complexity.

The 1985 National Assessment of Educational Progress (NAEP) study identified approximately 20 percent of the population as needing basic literacy help, comparable to Level I of the NALS. When Level I and Level II scores are combined, the 1993 NALS shows that nearly 50 percent of the population lack the skills necessary to read, write, and compute at a level adequate to achieve the economic, personal, and social life to which they may aspire. Although the interpretation of the NALS is still being widely debated, it is clear that too many adults in this country lack some of the necessary literacy skills.[2]

Why have the numbers of functional illiterates increased so significantly? One reason is simply that the level of literacy needed for mere survival has increased dramatically. At one time—as late as the early 1900s—an adult needed only to be able to write his or her name in order to be considered literate. In today's high-tech world, even a fifth- or sixth-grade literacy level is not enough to successfully perform most jobs. And there are fewer and fewer jobs available that can be satisfied by the minimal literacy skills once deemed adequate for a large variety of occupations.

Another reason for the rise of illiteracy in this country is that our population has increased at an incredible rate and there are simply many more people. Add to this the hundreds of thousands of new immigrants coming each year from countries where English is not spoken, even by the educated, and you have a very high rate of illiteracy. Compounding the problem even further, some of these immigrants lack basic literacy skills in their native language as well as in English.

There has also been a noticeable change in the attitudes of many immigrants about becoming literate in English. It once was the dream of every immigrant to learn English and to become assimilated into the new American culture as soon as possible. Now, many new immigrants, and even second and third generation immigrants, are more concerned with preserving the culture and language of their native country than with becoming assimilated. This statement should not be taken as a criticism of their concern but merely as an observation of how this change in attitude has impacted the rising numbers of adults with less than adequate English literacy skills.

WHY IS FAMILY LITERACY THE ANSWER?

As early as 1928, Jessie Charters, a leading advocate of parent education and considered by many to be the first professor of adult education in the United States, warned that the trend toward institutionalization of the education of children removed it from the responsibility of the parent. She felt strongly that this trend disrupted the family and would hasten its disintegration, while noting that the family was already seriously threatened by the new American economy and emphasis on industrialization.[3]

> Literacy level is not the only determiner of success in our society but lack of literacy is certainly linked to unemployment and underemployment, poverty and crime. As a nation we spend billions on education but even more on unemployment, welfare, police, prisons and jails. What we fail to provide for in the emerging literacy needs of our children, we pay for tenfold in the resulting myriad of social and educational problems directly resulting from or related to the school failures of our youth.[4]

Recent research has indicated that the single most important factor in determining the life chances of children is the level of educational attainment of the parents, particularly the mother. In his report *Making the Nation Smarter: The Intergenerational Transfer of Cognitive Ability* (1989), Tom Sticht found that "the major source of cognitive ability is the social environment into which the child is born and reared. It is this environment that provides the basic tools of thought, language, concepts and the means and motivation for 'intellectual' activities."[5] In addition, the 1985 NAEP study found that "youngsters whose parents are functionally illiterate are twice as likely as their peers to be functionally illiterate."

Supporting the emerging literacy needs of children can be a goal of the parent/primary caregiver as in Oakland Public Library's FFL program.

In his article "Adult Education for Family Literacy" (1995), Sticht reminds us that "the family is each society's first and most basic educational institution."[6] He also notes the stand taken by the United Nations in announcing 1994 as the International Year of the Family: "[L]iteracy is a prime conditioner of the ability of families to adapt, survive and even thrive in rapidly changing circumstances."[7]

At the same time that researchers have been noting the close correlation of reading scores in children and the reading skills, or lack thereof, of the parent(s); theories of education and reading acquisition have been embracing the whole language method as an effective and efficient way to extend and enhance reading skills in most children. This method may involve addressing the whole child and his or her needs and wants, while at the same time teaching reading based in literature rather than as an isolated skill or as a series of isolated skills. Whole language is most effective, however, when used as a component of a program that also includes phonics and other skill-based approaches. When the whole language/whole child approach is extended only slightly, we have the "whole family" concept used by family literacy programs.

Family literacy builds on the strengths of the family by helping the parents or primary caregivers to understand the impact that they have on their children. Many adults today feel helpless to make a difference for their children, but through family literacy programs they begin to conceptualize the vital role they play and to make conscious decisions about the legacies that they will pass on to their children. Few, if any, of these adults wish to pass on a legacy of illiteracy or crime or poverty. However, many adults fail to recognize their ability to control the legacy that they do pass on through their conscious and decisive efforts.

Because it is clear that interventive programs that prevent illiteracy are not only cheaper but more effective than programs that are developed later to "cure the problem," the model of family literacy begins to make even more sense. This model helps the provider intervene before literacy problems develop in the child and enables the adult to develop the reading, writing, and computation skills needed or desired.

Additionally, when family literacy is offered in a warm, positive, and nurturing environment, it not only becomes fun and enjoyable for all members of the family and the program staff, but enhances and expands positive, familial bonding.

Few literacy programs stay with a family forever, but library-based family literacy programs help all members of the program to leave or graduate with the recognition of a strong, positive legacy of resources that will be with them for life—literacy, libraries, and the family.

NOTES

1. *The State of Literacy in America: Estimates at the Local State and National Levels.* 1998. Washington, DC: National Institute for Literacy.
2. "Second Look at the U.S. Adult Literacy Survey." 1994. *Reading Today* (December 1993/January 1994): 10.

3. Lee Karlovic. 1993. "Jessie Allen Charters: A Voice for Our Times." *Adult Learning* 4, no. 5 (May/June): 13-14, 26.

4. Carole Talan. 1994 "Family Literacy Makes ene: Families That Read Together Succeed." *The Bottom Line* 7, nos. 3/4 (Winter/Spring): 46 -51.

5. Tom Sticht and Barbara McDonald. 1989. *Making the Nation Smarter: The Intergenerational Transfer of Cognitive Ability.* University Park, Penn.: Institute for the Study of Adult Literacy, Pennsylvania State University.

6. ———. 1995. *Adult Education for Family Literacy* (November/December): 23.

7. Ibid.

2 WHO IS OFFERING PROGRAMS?

> Jennifer, a family literacy child in Butte County, California, struggled in her first two years of school. Her father, an adult literacy student, read the Family Library books to her nightly, and eventually, Jennifer began reading the books on her own. At the May Storytime, after just one year in the library's program, Jennifer announced proudly that her teacher had moved her ahead a full grade in reading!
>
> —Jeanette Richards, former literacy coordinator, Butte County (Calif.) Library

Although not new as a concept, large, widespread, and successful family literacy programs and initiatives such as the one Jennifer attended in Butte County are still relatively recent. This chapter will briefly describe nine of the more popular and successful ones.

NINE FAMILY LITERACY PROGRAMS

BOSTON UNIVERSITY FAMILY LITERACY PROGRAM

One of the early family literacy programs in the United States was that developed by Ruth Nickse at Boston University (BU) in 1984. Nickse had long held an interest in adult literacy and is the person responsible for the development of the external degree diploma for adults.

In 1984, Nickse began to realize that many adults were unable or unwilling to support the education of their children because of their own lack of literacy and/or memories of fear and embarrassment associated with school. Motivated by an initial desire to overcome this barrier for adults and with a desire to develop a model program for work-study students as literacy tutors, the teachers and staff at BU developed their Collaborations for Literacy program. In a departure from traditional adult education, Nickse and her staff viewed the "at risk" child and the "at risk" parent as a learning unit and sought to provide an interrelated learning opportunity that would be motivational for the parent and interventive for the child.

Collaborations for Literacy: An Intergenerational Reading Project consisted of "one-on-one tutoring for native English-speaking adults with poor reading skills who were willing to improve their own skills through reading to and with children ages four to eleven."[1] The program was a collaborative effort of the university, a community school, a branch of the Boston Public Library, and an adult literacy organization. Although the primary focus of the BU program remained that of providing adults with the basic literacy skills that they needed, the use of the children's books became an important incentive and motivator for the adults to not only attend their tutoring sessions but to stay with the program. This program was to become the basic model around which many other family literacy programs were to later develop.

HANDEL-GOLDSMITH'S LITERACY INTERVENTION FOR FAMILIES

Ruth Handel and Ellen Goldsmith, while teaching developmental reading at New York City Technical College of the City University of New York in 1986, conceptualized a program for their students to enhance their literacy through assisting them in developing reading relationships with their children using quality children's literature. A grant proposal was submitted to the Taconic Foundation and was funded. The objective of this Parent Readers Program as it was called, was to develop the reading abilities of both generations, adults and children. The program consisted of a workshop series in which adult caregivers, including parents and siblings, learned how to read and discuss children's literature of different genres and to transfer their new skills and enjoyment to children in their families.

In fall 1987, the Handel-Goldsmith model was inaugurated in a public school in Newark, New Jersey, as a collaboration between Montclair State University and the Newark public schools. Called Partnership for Family Reading, it was instituted in 34 Newark schools, and many more schools throughout the country have since participated. Although this program did not directly address the many issues concerning parenting that later models were to emphasize, parenting issues of many kinds were indirectly explored through the children's books that were used. These two innovative ladies also published the first family literacy curriculum in 1990, *Family Reading: An Intergenerational Approach to Literacy.*[2]

In 1990, the Center for Intergenerational Reading was established at New York Technical College and Reading Starts with Us was developed. Also based on the Handel-Goldsmith model, Reading Starts with Us trains teachers to provide a workshop series that achieves both family literacy and parent involvement. An evaluation by the Institute for Literacy Studies at Lehman College found that Reading Starts with Us connects home and school, fosters parent-teacher collaboration and promotes parent collaboration.

To date, more than fifty daycare, Head Start, and public schools have instituted Reading Starts with Us programs. A 1997 collaboration with the Brooklyn Public Library enhanced this program by adding a major library component. Librarians in Brooklyn provided booktalks at staff development workshop sessions and hosted Saturday events for the families. A Reading Starts with Us kit, coauthored by Ellen Goldsmith and AnnMarie Tevlin, is available from Scholastic.

NATIONAL CENTER FOR FAMILY

In 1986 the Kentucky Department of Education, led by Sharon Darling, embarked on a mission to develop a family literacy model that would work in their rural, isolated areas where illiteracy rates were high and transportation was a major problem. What developed in response to this challenge was a family literacy model that proved highly successful and was to become the catalyst for the creation of the National Center for Family Literacy.

The original program was called PACE (Parent and Child Education). This model evolved and was later referred to as the Kenan Model (after the Kenan Family Trust, which funded the expansion of the model within and beyond Kentucky). This model consists of basically five components:

- adult literacy and GED preparation;
- emerging literacy activities for the child;
- parent and child interaction time together (called PACT);
- parenting discussions and development of basic parenting skills;
- and parent involvement in the child's school as volunteers in a variety of positions.

Programs were based initially in the elementary schools in which the families' preschoolers would enroll when they reached five years of age. In some communities the children and parent (usually the mother) were bused to the school three or four days per week for a full six-hour day. A healthy breakfast and lunch were provided at the site.

Later the National Center for Family Literacy (NCFL) became a private, nonprofit corporation with the intent to advocate for family literacy on a national level. It also provides training and technical assistance to program providers, conducts research to expand the knowledge base of family literacy, funds selected program models, and disseminates information to literacy providers; federal, state, and local policymakers; and interested organizations.

Among the programs administered by NCFL are the Kenan Family Literacy Project and the Toyota Family Literacy effort. With large grants from major corporations such as Toyota, contracts with such agencies as the Bureau of Indian Affairs, and foundations such as the Kenan Family Trust and the Lila Wallace/Readers Digest Fund, the center has played a major role in family literacy throughout the country.[3]

NCFL has been instrumental in raising the awareness of the need for family literacy and Sharon Darling has been its powerful spokesperson and advocate. Partially because of the work and visibility of NCFL, Title II—Adult Education and Literacy Act was authorized by Congress in 1998. It is also known as the "Adult Education and Family Literacy Act," and provides federal adult education funding for family literacy services for the first time in our history.

BARBARA BUSH FOUNDATION

The Barbara Bush Foundation was announced in March 1989 with former first lady Mrs. Bush serving as the foundation's honorary chairperson. The foundation

- supports grants to establish intergenerational dimensions in existing successful literacy programs;
- provides seed money for community planning of family literacy activities;
- trains volunteers and teachers;
- recognizes and honors volunteers, teachers, and students in successful programs;
- provides help to those interested in establishing family literacy efforts; and
- published a book, *First Teachers*, to highlight successful family literacy programs.

Although no library family literacy program was featured in *First Teachers*,[4] mention was made of the fact that libraries are often involved in this programming. The book also noted that of the 224 library literacy projects funded by LSCA (Library Services and Construction Act) in fiscal year 1988, 11 provided family literacy activities.[5] In addition, many public libraries annually submit applications to the foundation for grants for local programs.

In addition to providing grants to numerous family literacy programs throughout the country, the foundation also developed two statewide family literacy initiatives, one in Maine and one in Texas. The "First Lady's Family Literacy Initiative for Texas" is designed to complement important school reform efforts at the PreK–third grade levels. Grants of up to $20,000 are awarded to applicants who focus on building literacy skills for parents or other caregivers and young children. Priority for these one-time-only grants is given to projects that collaborate with public schools or school districts.

ILLINOIS SOS FAMILY LITERACY PROJECTS

In fiscal years 1993 and 1994, the Illinois Secretary of State Literacy Office/Illinois State Library used federal funding to establish the state's first Secretary of State (SOS) Family Literacy projects. Because of the early success of these projects, legislation was initiated that would provide permanent state funding for family literacy. Grants are awarded annually and applicants are required to demonstrate the involvement of three service providers: an adult literacy provider, an organization serving children at risk, and a public library.

The SOS family literacy grant projects must provide adult educational services to increase the literacy level of the parent; children's educational services to increase the appropriate developmental skills of the children; library services to increase the families' abilities to use the library and their comfort level with its use; and parent-child activities which integrate the learning of the parents and the children. Grants up to $35,000 are awarded annually to agencies in Illinois that apply as collaborative partners. Although a public library must be a partner in any funded project, the primary applicant may be a school district or another partner in the project.

WHAT ARE LIBRARIES DOING?

Nationally many public libraries are actively involved with family literacy. Libraries as varied and far apart as Los Angeles Public Library in California and Scotland County Memorial Library in North Carolina are providing specific family literacy services to their communities. Just how many family literacy programs exist in libraries across our county is not known, but Debra Wilcox Johnson and Leslie Edmund's publication *Family Literacy Library Programs: Models of Service* (1990) published by the Iowa State Library[6] does an excellent job of describing a variety of types of existing programs as well as making suggestions related to developing a local program. Mary Sommerville, president of the American Library Association 1996/97, also contributed to the increase in interest in family literacy through her "Kids Can't Wait" campaign to involve libraries in the service of children.

Some library literacy services are funded solely by local resources or by individual donations. Many local programs, however, were once funded by federal grants, primarily LSCA Title VI or LSCA Title I. The new LSTA (Library Services and Technology Act) Title I now funds some literacy programs in public libraries. However, because there are no longer specific funds for literacy as that there were in LSCA Title

VI, not as many library literacy programs are being funded with these federal dollars. Libraries applying for LSTA funds for literacy must compete with all types of library programs and services for the scarce resources provided through this act.

In 1987–88, the New York State Library used a portion of their LSCA monies to fund 17 library systems up to $50,000 to develop a family reading program—107 libraries of all sizes in 52 counties were involved in this project. According to Anne Simon and Carol Sheffer of the New York State Library, each of the 17 systems took its own unique approach to family literacy and developed programs around local needs and resources. Each of these programs is briefly described in the Spring 1989 issue of *INTERFACE*, a publication of the New York State Library.

BELL ATLANTIC/AMERICAN LIBRARY ASSOCIATION FAMILY LITERACY PROJECT

Bell Atlantic and the American Library Association began a public-private partnership in family literacy in 1990 in the mid-Atlantic region. With a grant from the Bell Atlantic Charitable Foundation, the ALA initiated a project to fund family literacy programs in local libraries within the Bell Atlantic area. The goal of the project was to encourage local partnerships among libraries, adult education and literacy providers, and businesses to develop library-based family literacy programs.

Twenty-five library programs were funded the first year. Twelve projects were continued, and 13 new projects were begun in the second year. In its third year, eight new projects were funded and matching dollars were provided for four existing projects. In the course of four years, over one million dollars was contributed to this effort by Bell Atlantic.[7]

This cooperative venture is just one example of the types of local, business, and foundation support that can be made available to libraries. For more information about this program, see the booklet *Library-Based Family Literacy Projects* (1991), published by the American Library Association.

CALIFORNIA'S FAMILIES FOR LITERACY

The first statewide, state-funded family literacy initiative was passed by the California legislature in 1986, but it remained unfunded for more than a year. The California legislature funded this program beginning in July 1988 and the public library-based Families for Literacy (FFL) program began.

FFL provides state local assistance dollars each year from the California Library Services Act so that local libraries already providing adult literacy services (usually through the state-funded California Li-

A Families for Literacy "lawn party" at San Rafael Public Library.

brary Literacy Services [CLLS]) can extend their services to include direct services to the families of adult learners who have a preschool child. Once qualified by having a preschool child, all members of the eligible family are included in these family literacy programs. The CLLS and FFL are both components of the California Literacy Campaign, a statewide, public library-based literacy initiative which was created in 1984.

One of the goals of the FFL programs is to introduce adult learners and their families to the value and joy of reading as a family. These programs are built on the premise that children who are talked to and read to by adults develop greater language skills, learn to read better, and have an improved opportunity to become more successful learners as a result, thus breaking the cycle of illiteracy.

It is not the intention of FFL to have parents teach their children to read, but to recognize and foster the vital roles that parents can play in preparing children for lifetimes of enjoyment and success in reading. The programs recognize the fact that in order to achieve lasting and long-term effects for the children, the literacy skills, attitudes, and habits of the adult must be changed. It is mandatory that the adult (any primary caregiver in the family or extended family) both need and receive literacy services for the family to be eligible to participate.

To meet the minimum requirements for providing services with FFL funding, a library must

- provide free gift books for the families to build home libraries (over 30,000 books were distributed in FY 97/98);
- hold meetings in libraries and introduce the families to the resources and services available (over 1,668 held in FY 97/98);
- provide storytelling, word games, and other enjoyable reading-oriented activities for families;
- encourage the use of children's books for tutoring and language experience stories from the family programs as adult literacy instructional materials;
- teach parents how to select books and why and how to read aloud to children;
- provide services that enhance full family participation and that foster a family environment for reading;
- help parents gain access to information on parenting, child care, health, nutrition, family-life education, and so forth.

Over 2,650 families with more than 5,375 children participated in FFL in the 1997/98 fiscal year.

FFL is viewed as a joint effort of Children's Services and Adult Literacy Services in the local public library. In addition, local programs are encouraged to form partnerships with other agencies and organizations in their communities to better serve these families. Partners often include Head Start, Even Start, Healthy Start, low-income daycare providers, elementary schools, adult schools, detention facilities, homeless shelters, rehabilitation centers, and healthcare providers, for example.

In the first year of this initiative, 21 library jurisdictions established FFL programs. This program has expanded until in FY 1998/99 programs were funded in 59 public library jurisdictions with an additional five jurisdictions providing family literacy programs funded through other sources.

A 1996/97 evaluation of the FFL program was conducted by Barbara McDonald of San Diego. Dr. McDonald is a noted researcher in adult and family literacy and has coauthored a number of studies with Tom Sticht. She found the FFL program to be highly successful and cost effective. Improvements in family literacy attitudes and habits as measured by the FFL Parent Survey (Appendix H) were statistically significant after six to nine months' involvement in the program. In

Family literacy programs in libraries meet the literacy needs of all members of a family. Here family members of all ages receive free books in National City, California.

addition, McDonald noted that she was very impressed with the library-based programs and would like to further explore why the improvements and changes experienced by families in library programs are greater than those in families she had studied and measured in community colleges. Although she and this author speculated that the one-on-one tutoring and the wealth of resources in the library were at least partially responsible for the higher success of FFL, plans are to engage in a three-year study of the program from 1999–2002 to more fully investigate this.

SAN QUENTIN'S F.A.T.H.E.R.S. PROGRAM

In 1993, using federal LSCA Title I funds from the California State Library, this author conceived and instituted a two-year pilot family literacy project named F.A.T.H.E.R.S. (Fathers As Teachers: Helping, Encouraging, Reading, Supporting) at San Quentin Prison near San

Francisco, California. The aim of this program was to help incarcerated men maintain positive contact with their children and to take responsibility for their roles as teachers and models for children. The program also helps the inmates to view the library as a lifetime resource for free books and materials for themselves and their families. It provides them with a valuable means of reconnecting with their families and their community upon release.

Similar to California's Families for Literacy program, after which it was modeled, the F.A.T.H.E.R.S. program has three major components:

- literacy and parenting instruction;
- interactive storytimes;
- gift books.

As part of a two-year pilot, the F.A.T.H.E.R.S. curriculum was introduced into a variety of different classes and settings at the prison before finding its niche in the prerelease program. It was here that the curriculum was most effective because the men in the classes were facing the exciting but terrifying prospect of release and reentry back into their families and neighborhoods, and thus into the lives of children.

The F.A.T.H.E.R.S. program curriculum uses children's literature and interactive discussion, rather than confrontational or advice-giving lectures, to raise consciousness and change behaviors in five ways:

- Break the cycle of incarceration and low literacy.
- Promote conscious positive role modeling as fathers and father figures.
- Educate fathers to become their child's first teacher.
- Empower children with literacy skills and with the self-esteem necessary to negotiate on their own behalf.
- Instruct fathers to use children's books to teach their children and to make personal connections with them. (Curtis, 1995:7)[8]

A 13-lesson curriculum was developed as part of this pilot. The *F.A.T.H.E.R.S. Program Guide*, written by project coordinator Jane Curtis, not only provides the full curriculum but also contains clear, easy guides to using the curriculum. An annotated bibliography of children's literature appropriate to a family literacy project accompanies the curriculum. A sample lesson from this guide can be found in Appendix A. This guide is available from the California State Library Foundation in Sacramento.

Because of the success of the curriculum and its popularity with both the inmates and custodians at San Quentin, this program has become part of the ongoing curriculum of the prerelease program. Positive feedback of the results of the program has been given by the inmates themselves; the children for whom they are fathers or father figures; and from wives, girlfriends, sisters, and other relatives in whose homes the released men later resided.

HEAD START/LIBRARY FAMILY LITERACY PARTNERSHIP

In November 1989 a symposium on the potential of partnerships between libraries and other agencies serving children and families was held at the Library of Congress. One result of this symposium was an Interagency Agreement between the Center for the Book in the Library of Congress and the Head Start Bureau. Forty participants representing more than 30 states met for a three-day planning meeting in 1992 to develop the concept and goals for the partnership as well as specific guidelines for achieving these.

By fall 1993, the Head Start/Library Partnership video with resource book and training guide was completed and shipped to Head Start grantees and delegate agencies. Multistate regional meetings of Head Start leaders and children's librarians were held in three locations, beginning with Sacramento, California, then Richmond, Virginia, and finally Topeka, Kansas. These meetings introduced the concept of the partnership, developed an understanding and appreciation for the needs and resources of each partner, provided training in the use of the materials, and provided for interaction among the participants for creating and planning for the partnership in their own states.

The partnership and regional meetings/trainings were so successful that the Association of Youth Museums asked to become a partner. Museums were welcomed into the partnership and added another exciting component to the resources available in many communities. A single state training model employing the new, expanded partnership was presented in Florida in February 1995 and another multistate regional meeting was held in Minnesota in April.

When the partnership was funded again in 1995/96, specific, indepth workshops were presented in Texas, Arizona/New Mexico, and Colorado. Some states, such as California, have also funded local model programs that could be replicated by other libraries. Oakland Public Library received a 1997/98 LSCA Title I grant and developed and tested a successful model that gradually will be spread to other California libraries using small LSTA Title I grants. Called "Books for Wider Horizons," the Oakland project trains and supports volunteer story readers for Head Start Centers throughout the city and is managed by Children's Services at the library.

The Head Start/Library Partnership Project and its materials and training have been successful. They have resulted not only in the training sessions sponsored by the project itself, but also many additional training sessions that have begun from these. The state and local partnerships created by this project have been very effective in developing the shared resources that benefit both the Head Start families, their local public libraries, and their community children's museums.

Family literacy programs in some form have been around for many years. Although this chapter has described a few programs and initiatives, many others can be found throughout our nation as well as in other countries. It is not the intent of this book to go into detail on the various programs and models. However, more information on a variety of different family literacy programs is readily available on the Internet, through the National Institute for Literacy, and through the National Center for Family Literacy.

NOTES

1. Ruth S. Nickse and Nancy Englander. 1985. "At Risk Parents: Collaboration for Literacy, An Intergenerational Reading Project." *Equity and Choice* 1, no. 3 (Spring): 11–18.
2. Ellen Goldsmith and Ruth D. Handel. 1990. *Family Reading: An Intergenerational Approach to Literacy*. Syracuse, N.Y.: New Readers Press.
3. Jack A. Brizius and Susan A. Foster. 1993. *Generation to Generation, Realizing the Promise of Family Literacy*. Ypsilanti, Mich.: High/Scope Press.
4. *First Teachers*. 1989. Washington, D.C.: The Barbara Bush Foundation for Family Literacy.
5. Debra Wilcox Johnson and Leslie Edmunds. 1990. *Family Literacy Library Programs: Models of Service*. Des Moines, Ia.: Iowa State Library.
6. Ibid.
7. Margaret Monsour and Carole Talan. 1991. *Library-Based Family Literacy Projects*. Chicago: American Library Association.
8. Curtis, Jane. 1999. *F.A.T.H.E.R.S. Program Guide*. Sacramento, Calif.: California State Library Foundation.

3 COULD YOU BRING A FAMILY LITERACY PROGRAM TO YOUR LIBRARY?

A family from the Willows Public Library (Calif.) was moving across the U.S. to gain employment. The family came by the library to say good-bye. The children were very apprehensive about moving. One young boy said he'd go to the library in his new neighborhood the first thing to see if they had his favorite books and maybe make some new friends. His experience in the library's family literacy program had been so positive that he had learned that the library is a friend and a good place to go, no matter where you are.
—Susan Domeniginhi, literacy coordinator,
Willows (Calif.) Public Library

ADVANTAGES OF A LIBRARY-BASED FAMILY LITERACY PROGRAM

There are many advantages to basing a family literacy program in a library. "Library-based" refers to the fact that a library is at the core of the program. It can, but not necessarily does, mean that the library is the primary provider of all the family literacy services. A program can be library-based even when the library is just one of many partners in a collaborative.

Some of the reasons family literacy efforts benefit from being library-based are

- That's where the books are!
- That's where people who are crusaders for reading are!
- The public library is a safe haven—nonthreatening to parents and to children—providing a positive setting without an institutional stigma attached.
- Librarians love books and reading and avidly promote and model the joy of reading to others.
- Other wonderful materials are found at the library and families who go there can access these, such as videos, books on tape, large-print books, and dictionaries.

- The public library is THE "life-long learning institution" which will never graduate or promote you out of its services; you can always use the library no matter how old or how young you are, how educated or uneducated.
- Libraries are community centers where individuals with all levels of education come for information.
- Libraries provide for the developmental literacy needs of children and of adults.
- Children who discover the world of reading at the library will continue to access it for the rest of their lives.
- Public libraries are FREE and in nearly every community!
- Many public libraries are open nights and weekends (even Sundays) so they are accessible to working parents.
- Most public libraries provide entertaining, informative, and fun programs for children as well as the entire family.
- Children and adults can correlate their books with each other by subject or genre, thus encouraging family discussions and experiences.
- Public libraries are nondiscriminatory. They have "something for everyone!"

CONVINCING YOUR LIBRARY ABOUT LITERACY

Not all librarians are convinced that the public library is the appropriate place for literacy, whether adult or family. But, convincing your local library of the value of and need for getting involved in literacy is one of the first critical steps to implementing a program. The following are some of the reasons that may be used in developing needed "in-house" support.

PROGRESSING FROM PASSIVE TO ACTIVE COMMUNITY INVOLVEMENT

Libraries are too often seen as passive participants in their communities. There are some notable exceptions, but the general view is that the library sits there quietly waiting for the members of the community to decide that they need information or a book. These community members are then expected to know that the library is available and to come forward with their request.

Involvement with literacy, however, changes the role of the library into a very active and visible one within the community. Literacy requires community assessment, outreach, and publicity. It means becoming known in the community as a place to come to resolve problems, to interact with other community members, to deal with issues and people. Literacy involvement demands that the library go to the people and be known by the people. A library involved in literacy is a social institution working to help solve a social problem!

DEVELOPING POSITIVE PUBLIC RELATIONS

Literacy also brings good public relations to the library. People who have never thought about library issues suddenly realize the importance of the library to the entire community. A perfect example of the impact of this very aspect can be found in an event in California.

The California State Library had been working to pass legislation to fund an annex to the State Library in Sacramento. This was desperately needed as the lack of proper facilities had already caused the loss of some valuable collections to mold. At that time the battle was a difficult one because of a severe state deficit and recent budget cuts.

One of California's strongest assemblymen and a close confidant to the then governor came out in support of the bill and was instrumental in getting it passed in the Assembly and into the Senate. That assemblyman had never been a particular supporter of the library, but he was a committed supporter of literacy and had become familiar with the State Library and its staff through his work with its California Literacy Campaign. He was not an opponent of libraries, he had just never been a vocal supporter. However, because of the involvement of the State Library in *literacy*, this assemblyman proved to be the pivotal influence in the passage of the annex bill and he continued his support into other arenas of library service. Similar scenarios have been played out time and time again, both on the state and the local levels.

CREATING NEW LIBRARY USERS

Another reason at the heart of why public libraries must be involved in literacy is the fact that it does increase the number of people in the community who are able to use and do use library services. Librarians have a vested interest in literacy. It may be a long journey from new reader to regular library user, but adult literacy students are making that journey every day.

Additionally, involvement in family literacy programming in the library clearly leads to the development of information-seeking behaviors on the part of the adult learners and their families. California programs have found that library use for these participants is not only raised, but the ways in which they use the library are expanded.

A family from the Benicia (Calif.) Public Library exemplifies the way family literacy programs produce readers and library users. When

Family literacy programs make the public library more visible and help it to serve the needs of all members of the community, as at Escondido (CA) Public Library's literacy fair.

the mother first entered the program her youngest child was three years old and had no interest in books and reading. Over the next two years, the gift books he received became more and more precious to him. The family soon became frequent library patrons, attending the regular children's programming and checking out books.

After the child entered kindergarten the family was no longer involved in the literacy program but the mother continued to drop by and report on her progress. Once the mother arrived with her now six-year-old son just in time for a family literacy program. They were invited to stay but did not receive a gift book. The mother understood, but the six-year-old really wanted a book.

The family literacy coordinator found that the child had his library card with him so she took him to the children's section and told him to pick out a group of books to take home. He understood that these books had to be returned, but he was just as thrilled as when he received gift books. "For this little boy, receiving gift books had gradually transformed from being uninteresting, to the excitement of a new possession, to an excitement about reading and libraries" wrote Sandy Kirkpatrick, FFL coordinator and children's librarian in her FFL annual report.

A great deal of personal attention is required in family literacy. Much one-on-one work, tutor and staff encouragement, and individual modeling for parents in how to read and relate to their children are needed. The work here is very staff intensive, but the payoff is in the fact that not just one person but the entire family benefits. Often the family is a large one, and as many as five to ten individuals or more can be reached through a single family. These benefits are compounded with each succeeding generation. And, an investment in family literacy ensures that the entire family will come to know the library as a resource.

FULFILLING YOUR LIBRARY'S MISSION STATEMENT

Most of you need look no further than the mission statement of your own library to find the strongest arguments for a library-based family literacy program. The majority of public library mission statements, though they vary in the specific wording, contain the following goals:

- to provide all types of reading material for all ages of people;
- to provide ease of access to this material;
- to provide life-long learning opportunities; and
- to provide for the informational and educational needs of the diverse populations within their community.

Offering adult and family literacy services at a public library is one way that libraries can fulfill their missions. Without literacy services, a great many people in the community cannot take advantage of, or even begin to understand, the resources available in their library. If libraries do not fulfill their mission to the serve all the members of their communities, they become elite institutions serving the educated elite. It has been said that "illiteracy is the greatest form of censorship" and I have yet to meet the librarian who believes in censorship!

I was very much surprised when still new to the library world to discover that not everyone is a library user. Indeed, many people living within a short walking distance of their local library do not have library cards, and many more who do have cards are not regular users. Even more astounding is the fact that a number of people have no idea of the type and variety of services available at their local public library, and that these services are FREE!

A few years ago two of the VISTA volunteers from library programs in the San Diego area conducted a door-to-door canvas of low-income neighborhoods that the literacy programs had been trying to serve. They found that many of the families did not know what a library was or that libraries provided free services of any kind. Additionally, many did not know where their library was located, even when it was just a block away from their home.

ENHANCING COMMUNITY INVOLVEMENT

Finally, there is still yet another argument for library-based literacy. As adults develop their literacy skills, it is easier for them to become active and productive members of the communities in which they live. Oakland Public Library's 1997/98 FFL Final Report noted that one of their long-time students whose family was in the FFL program is now an employee in their adult literacy program. She has become a student leader, a community activist, and a strong advocate for FFL. She was selected as "Oakland's Mother of the Year" and was honored at a ceremony in the Rose Garden by the city and the mayor. She has become a more effective mother and community member because of her involvement in the library's family literacy program.

Providing literacy services merely serves to round out the relationship that libraries already have with their communities—that of providing for the personal and educational development of the individual—and ensures that *all* people can take full advantage of library and information services. And, if you choose to become involved with family literacy, you help to ensure that generations to come will also be able to take full advantage of the services of your library.

IT MAY NOT BE EASY

Some librarians fear involvement in literacy because they are concerned that they will be asked to do too much. Many are already overworked and this is a legitimate concern. If they are barely surviving now providing the traditional services, why should they take on more?

There may also be a fear of being overwhelmed by a new population that may look very different from the one they are used to. They may doubt their ability to address the needs of this new population as it begins to seek traditional library service. Language can be, and often is, an additional barrier.

Ruth Nickse, in her *The Noises of Literacy: An Overview of Intergenerational and Family Literacy Programs*, points out that

> new kinds of staffing and different trainings for librarians are needed to develop the expertise in children's and adult literacy and in understanding issues related to poverty and cultural differences of new library members. Programs aimed toward "at risk" families, newly

literate adults, adult literacy students, teen parents and educationally disadvantaged families have special staff needs as they both recruit new target populations (i.e., Chapter I parents) and conduct programs for them.[1]

Your library staff may have many of the same or different issues and concerns from those mentioned. It is important that you be prepared for this and actively solicit and address their concerns. Use all the statistics and information available to present the case and prepare your staff for library involvement in family literacy. Seek support from librarians who have already taken on family literacy as an ongoing service. They can speak from personal experience about the benefits to the library and to them personally.

NOTE

1. Ruth Nickse. 1989. *The Noises of Literacy: An Overview of Intergenerational and Family Literacy Programs.* Washington, D.C.: Paper commissioned by the Office of the Secretary of Education, U.S. Department of Education: (March 3): 21–22.

4 WHAT DOES YOUR COMMUNITY NEED?

Robert and Deborah H. were high school sweethearts in National City, California. They often met at the library because there were so few safe, quiet and comfortable places to meet without cost. They eventually married and the library staff encouraged them to enroll in their family literacy program (PATterns) after the birth of their first child as a means of enhancing their growing family bond as well as the educational future of their young son. They now have two sons with whom they read aloud every evening. According to Deborah, "My husband and I view PATterns as just that: it set a pattern, a foundation, for our family literacy. It taught us the importance of reading on a regular basis and techniques to enhance language development in our children." Deborah now works for the National City School District's Parents as Teachers program, working with other at-risk parents and demonstrating first hand her pattern for success.
—Beverly Whitcomb, FFL coordinator, National City (Calif.) Public Library

ASSESSING LITERACY NEEDS AND RESOURCES IN YOUR COMMUNITY

Before embarking on any family literacy effort, it is important that you first assess the need for and the availability of existing family literacy services in your community. Not every community needs the library to develop its family literacy initiative from scratch. You may discover in a community assessment that

- a family literacy program already exists in which the library needs only to become an active partner;
- many of the components of a good family literacy program are already present in the community and the library needs only to provide a mechanism for bringing the partners together;
- many of the components of a good family literacy program are already present in the community, and the library needs to serve not just as the catalyst for bringing them together but also as the key partner in the effort;
- none of the necessary components of family literacy are available in the community and that the library needs to set about

developing and providing the full range of services needed in a family literacy program.

According to Debra Wilcox Johnson in her *Fact Sheet on Needs Assessment* published in 1991 by the American Library Association as part of the Bell Atlantic-ALA Family Literacy Project, the three main planning categories with which libraries need to be concerned include identifying

- the nature of the problem and the extent of the need for services,
- the other agencies already serving the client group,
- the strengths and weaknesses of the library in relationship to the components of family literacy.

Your needs assessment is the first step in defining your project. It will help you determine who will be served, what specific needs are met or unmet, what is already being done to serve your clientele, who is doing it, and the barriers to overcome.

A needs assessment should be both quantitative and qualitative. Quantitative techniques might include general statistics available on literacy needs in your geographic area such as those available from the National Adult Literacy Survey (NALS). These can be accessed on the Internet at www.nifl.gov and on the individual home pages of the various state literacy resource centers and state departments of education. Census information can also be helpful in identifying the educational and ethnic makeup of a community and comparing that to broader literacy data. Surveys can also be used to collect quantitative information.

Qualitative information is also valuable. In order to gather this, a library might form a focus group made up of the low-literacy adults it already serves, or wishes to serve, and other local literacy providers and interested groups. Another approach involves seeking out key informants in a community and interviewing them. See Chapter 5, under Specific Steps For Creating Your Family Literacy Program, for more information on focus groups and key informants. Surveys can also be very helpful in obtaining qualitative information.

Assessing local literacy needs involves looking at adult literacy statistics including immigration patterns in your area. These young Asian children are part of a growing population in San Diego Public Library's FFL program.

FOUR STEPS TO ASSESSING COMMUNITY FAMILY LITERACY NEEDS

In 1988, this author wrote and published a *Literacy Needs Assessment* (LNA), a tool designed to aid a community in assessing its need for literacy services. The document was commissioned and published by Altrusa, International, and was commonly referred to as the LNA. United Way later borrowed from this model in developing its tool for the same purpose. This is a version of the original LNA updated and adapted slightly for family literacy.

> Step 1: Analysis of NALS and census data
> Step 2: Survey of Literacy Providers
> Step 3: Survey of Potential Client Families and Students
> Step 4: Survey of Other Service Providers

Completion of all four steps is recommended in order to most clearly identify both the need and the existing resources in a given community

Step 1: Analysis of NALS and census data

In 1988 the U.S. Congress directed the Department of Education to carry out an assessment of the literacy skills of American adults. The result was the National Adult Literacy Study (NALS), which provides the most comprehensive and statistically reliable source of data on adult literacy in the United States. Approximately 26,000 adults were interviewed in their own homes and a report was issued in 1993. A comprehensive description and review of the NALS, including information from the 12 states that also conducted concurrent state surveys (SALS), is available from the National Center for Educational Statistics on the World Wide Web at nces.ed.gov/nadlits/index.html.

Although the national data were significant and important, most individuals were primarily interested in what these statistics meant in their own states, counties, and cities. In response to this interest, the Department of Education asked researcher Stephen Reder of Portland State University to calculate synthetic estimates of adult literacy proficiency for those areas with adult populations over 5,000.[1] This information is now available from the Office of Vocational and Adult Education's Division of Adult Education and Literacy (OVAEL) and from the National Institute for Literacy (NIFL).[2]

Local adult literacy information from Reder's synthetic estimates is easily accessed in a searchable database on the World Wide Web. One can find more information about the NALS as well as search for spe-

One important component of family literacy programs is getting books to families for home libraries. Here children in National City (CA) pick out their books to take home.

cific local statistics at www.nifl.gov/reders/reder.htm. These estimates provide the best local information currently available; and a review and analysis of them should be the first step in a literacy needs assessment. It is anticipated that a new NALS study will be conducted early in the twenty-first century and will provide new, updated statistical data.

Although less accurate than the NALS data, certain census data can also be a significant indicator of literacy/illiteracy. This data is readily available to you from the local census bureau or at your library.

According to the U.S. Department of Education in its report *Adult Illiteracy Estimates for States* (1985) the following census data can be an indicator of low levels of literacy within a community:

1. Number of people with completed education level of
    a. grade 0–4
    b. grade 5–8
    c. grade 9–11 (This data, however, can be misleading as many

high school graduates do not have a literacy level commensurate with their completed educational level.)
2. Number of people of foreign birth.
3. Recency of immigration for non-natives.
4. Number of people 60 years and older.
5. Number of adults 18+ who do *not* speak English well.
6. Number of Black adults. (In many communities this is no longer a reliable indicator. Look instead at the number of adults in a variety of potentially at-risk populations such as Hispanic, Black, and Southeast Asian)
7. Number who live below the poverty level.

Be very cautious about using census data. The information found there should serve only as an initial indicator. It is taken every ten years and drastic changes can occur in a community over that span of time. Additionally, many illiterates and non-English-speaking immigrants are not even included in the census because they fear having their illiteracy uncovered or their lack of appropriate papers discovered.

Step 2: Survey of Literacy Providers
The following survey has been developed for use with service providers within your community. The collection of this information should help you to establish a broad view of present resources as well as an idea of the areas of weakness or limitations within these resources.
It is recommended that the survey be completed by the following:

1. Adult schools, adult vocational programs, workplace literacy sites
2. Continuation schools (high schools that specialize in employed and special-needs young adults)
3. Community colleges
4. Head Start and Even Start
5. Community-based literacy programs
6. Library or other volunteer literacy programs
7. Daycare and childcare providers
8. Preschools
9. Anyone answering *yes* to question #9 on the survey of the Questionnaire for Providers of Services Other Than Literacy, which is any service provider who refers clients to literacy service providers (page 48).

Family Literacy Services Survey for Literacy Providers

Name of Agency _____

Agency Address _____

_____ Zip _____

Agency Phone _____

Person Completing Survey _____

    Title _____

Family literacy is made up of four basic components. Please check any and all of these component services which your agency presently provides:

_____ Adult literacy services

_____ Emerging literacy services for children

_____ Intergenerational literacy services

_____ Parenting services

1.   Approximately how many clients do you serve?

    _____ at any given time   _____ per year   _____ information not available

2.   How many clients in the following ethnic groups have you served during the past 12 months?

    _____ White   _____ Native Americans

    _____ Black   _____ Asian/Pacific Islander

    _____ Hispanic   _____ information not available

    _____ Other, please specify _____

3.   When are your services available?

Day(s) of week   **Times**

_____ Monday–Friday   _____

_____ Saturday   _____

_____ Sunday   _____

_____ determined by client/staff

4.   Are there any charges for participation in your program or for the materials you use?

_____ yes _____ no

If yes, what is your fee structure for services or materials costs? _____

_____

_____

5.   Are there eligibility criteria (unemployment status, AFDC, JTPA, residency, age, etc.) for your literacy services?

_____ yes _____ no

If yes, please explain _____

_____

_____

6.   Is there a waiting list of clients to receive your services?

_____ yes _____ no

If yes, what is the average wait?

_____ days _____ weeks _____ months

7.   In what zip code areas or community neighborhoods do most of your clients reside? _____

_____

8. Which of the following might potential clients perceive as barriers to participation in your program?

_____ time/day services offered   _____ instructional level

_____ fees or material costs   _____ stigma of illiteracy

_____ other eligibility requirements   _____ childcare issues

_____ location of services   _____ transportation

_____ lack of awareness of services   _____ privacy issue

_____ degree of individual attention

_____ other. Please specify _____

_____

9. Which of the following would help you to do a better job of providing the services that you now offer?

_____ resources   _____ volunteers

_____ staff   _____ recruitment

_____ equipment   _____ materials

_____ child care   _____ other. Please specify _____

_____

Complete all remaining questions which apply:

If you provide adult literacy services, complete questions 10–14.

If you provide literacy services for children, complete questions 15–17.

If you provide intergenerational literacy services, complete questions 18–19.

If you provide parenting services, complete questions 20–21.

10. What type of adult literacy services do you offer?

_____ ABE (Adult Basic Ed) only   _____ ESL/ESOL only   _____ LEP only

_____ ABE & ESL   _____ Adult Basic Math   _____ ABE & LEP

11. Please indicate how you provide literacy instruction:

    _____ one-to-one tutoring

    _____ large group   average # _____

    _____ small group   average # _____

    _____ computer-assisted instruction

12. Roughly what percent of your clients are

    _____ male   _____ female   _____ have children at home

13. Please rank in numerical order, from 1–5, the age groups most frequently served by your agency (1 = most frequent).

    _____ 16–19 years   _____ 46–59 years

    _____ 20–35 years   _____ 60 years and older

    _____ 36–45 years   _____ information not available

14. Please list the name, address, and phone number of other individuals or organizations that provide adult literacy services locally.

    Name   **Address**   **Phone #**

    _____

    _____

    _____

15. What type of services for children do you provide?

    _____ daycare   _____ preschool

    _____ evening childcare   _____ homework help

    _____ story hours   _____ other. Please specify _____

    _____

16. Please rank in numerical order, from 1–5, the age groups of children most frequently served by your agency. (1 = most frequent)

_____ 0–2 years   _____ 3–4 years

_____ 5 years   _____ 6–8 years

_____ 9–12 years   _____ 13 and older

                                                     _____ information not available

17. Please list the name, address, and phone number of other individuals or organizations that provide similar services for children locally.

Name   **Address**   **Phone #**

_____

_____

_____

18. What type of intergenerational programming or resources do you provide? Please describe

_____

_____

_____

_____

19. Please list the name, address, and phone number of other individuals or organizations that provide similar intergenerational services locally.

Name   **Address**   **Phone #**

_____

_____

_____

20. What type of parenting programming or resources do you provide?
Please describe

_____

_____

_____

_____

21. Please list the name, address, and phone number of other individuals or organizations that provide parenting services locally.

Name	**Address**	**Phone #**

Step 3: Survey of Potential Client Families and Students
Upon completion of Step 1, you have a general understanding of those areas in your community where, according to the NALS or the census data, the greatest need for literacy services exists. The objective of Step 3 is to select a sample (every 100th phone number, for instance) of adults living in these areas to be interviewed by phone.

This step is the most time consuming but can provide the most valuable information as it comes from the potential family literacy clients themselves. It should be noted that if there is an extensive Hispanic or other foreign language group in the community, the interviewer should be bilingual.

As an alternative to the phone interview, you might ask to visit students in existing adult programs to get a feel for the problem. They could be asked many of the same questions contained in the telephone survey.

Another option is to conduct a door-to-door survey in the communities identified in previous steps as having the greatest need. This is very time consuming but is more likely to yield broader cooperation.

Telephone Interview for Potential Client Families

Respondent Zip Code _____   Phone # _____

Date of Interview _____   Interviewer _____

Hello, I'm _____ with the _____(your group name here)_____.We are conducting a survey of families who live in this community. I need to speak to someone in your household who is 16 or over.

Hello, I'm _____ with the _____. We are conducting a survey of families who live in your community. We are collecting information about reading and writing experiences and skills. The information obtained from this study will be used to plan better education programs for our community.

All of the information that I will collect from you will be confidential. Would you be willing to take just a few minutes to answer some questions to help us with our survey?

1.   What is the highest grade of schooling which you completed? _____

     In the U.S.? _____

     Another country? _____

2.   Are you currently enrolled in school or taking any classes?

     _____ yes   _____ no (skip to Question 6)

3.   Are you a full-time or part-time student? _____ full _____ part

4.   How do you rate your educational experience?

     _____ excellent   _____ good   _____ fair   _____ poor   _____ very bad

5.   What type of classes are you taking?

     _____ job improvement   _____ job training

     _____ adult basic skills   _____ GED or high school equivalency

     _____ college   _____ other. Please explain _____

     _____

6. Were you born in the United States? _____yes _____no

7. What languages were spoken in your home when you were growing up?

   _____

   (if English is the only language, skip to Question 13)

8. What language do you usually speak now? _____

   With regard to English, how well do you _____?

	Very well	**well**	**fair**	**not well**	**not at all**
9. understand when spoken to?	_____	_____	_____	_____	_____
10. speak it?	_____	_____	_____	_____	_____
11. read it?	_____	_____	_____	_____	_____
12. write it?	_____	_____	_____	_____	_____

13. If you are not presently in school or taking classes, would you like to take classes someday?

   _____ yes (go Question 14)

   _____ no (go to Question 16)

14. What types of classes would interest you most?

   _____ reading   _____ college

   _____ writing   _____ computers

   _____ math   _____ present job improvement

   _____ GED   _____ new job training

15. What kind of class would you prefer?   _____ large class

   _____ small group   _____ one-on-one instruction

16. Why are you not taking classes now?

_____ no time   _____ bad location of classes

_____ wrong times   _____ fear of failure

_____ expensive   _____ childcare problems

_____ don't need   _____ transportation problems

_____ job prevents   _____ don't know about classes

_____ other. Please explain _____

17. Are you employed? _____

_____ yes (continue with Question 18)

_____ no (skip to Question 22)

18. What kind of work do you do? _____

19. Would you like a different or better job? _____

20. Are your reading skills good enough for the job you have? _____

21. Are your writing skills good enough for the job you have? _____
    (Skip to question 24)

22. Would you like a job? _____

23. Are your reading and writing skills good enough for the job you'd like to have? _____

24. Do you have preschool-age children living in your home? _____ Yes _____ No

    If yes, how many _____

25. Does anyone in your household read to the children? _____

26. Do you have school-age children living in your home? _____

    If yes, how many _____

27. Does anyone in your house help these children with schoolwork? _____

28. If a free program were available to help your children learn to read or improve their reading, would you take them to the program? _____

    Why/why not? _____

29. If **you** had to participate in this program with your children, would you go? _____

    Why/why not? _____

30. What is your ethnicity?

    _____ White   _____ African American

    _____ Hispanic   _____ Asian

    _____ Pacific Islander   _____ Native American

    _____ NA or Don't know

31. What is your sex? _____ male _____ female

32. What is your age? _____

33. What is your zip code? _____

Thank you so much for helping with this survey. Are there any questions that you would like to ask me?

Step 4: Survey of Other Service Providers

The following questionnaire has been developed for use with providers of social and personal services in your community other than literacy. The collection of this information should give you these providers' views of the literacy needs in your community, as well as a general sense of the resources that others recognize as available for meeting this need.

First contact the service provider by phone. Identify yourself, the name of your group, and a brief outline of your purpose in asking for their cooperation. Tell them that you will be sending a short questionnaire (deliver it personally if possible). Ask if they provide any literacy services for their clients. If the answer is "yes," send them a Family Literacy Services Survey for Literacy Providers also.

It is suggested that this questionnaire be completed by the following:

1. Social Services Department
2. Public Health Services Department, especially those divisions dealing with care to the elderly, in-home care, and any special services to immigrants/refugees
3. Doctors' and dentists' offices, clinics, hospital emergency rooms
4. Organizations providing assistance to refugees/immigrants
5. Planned Parenthood or family planning services
6. Employment Development Department, especially those divisions dealing with unemployed and disabled workers
7. Drug and alcohol rehabilitation programs
8. Mental health services/battered women's shelters/halfway houses
9. Probation and parole/inmate services
10. Churches and agencies, for example Goodwill Industries, Salvation Army, or Saint Vincent de Paul Society, that work with low-income families

Questionnaire for Providers of Services Other Than Literacy

Please fill in to the best of your ability. Answer with an estimate/percentage if you do not know exact numbers. Answer DO NOT KNOW if you have no estimate at all.

Name of Agency _____

Agency Address _____

_____ Zip _____

Agency Phone _____ Person Completing Survey _____

Title _____

1. How many different clients do you serve each year?

   _____

2. How many of these clients do not speak English well?

   _____

3. Of your total clientele, how many have difficulty filling out forms?

   _____

4. How many clients cannot fill out forms at all? (in other words, those who ask you to fill out; ask to take them home; bring along spouse or someone else to fill out)

   _____

5. According to your information, how many of these clients are presently receiving some form of literacy instruction?

   _____

6. In your opinion, how many of your clients who need literacy services would be interested in these services if they were readily available?

   _____

7. Which of the following are the most likely barriers to literacy services that affect your average client? (please rank in order with 1=most often)

    _____ child care   _____ cost of classes   _____ job interfere

    _____ transportation   _____ fear of failure

    _____ location of classes   _____ lack of interest

    _____ times of classes   _____ lack of awareness about services

    _____ other. Please explain _____

    _____

8. How many of your clients have children living in their homes?

    _____

9. Do you make referrals to your clients for literacy services?

    _____

    If yes, please list those places where you refer clients.

    _____

10. Would you make referrals to your clients for family literacy services?

    _____

11. Would you be interested in becoming a partner in a family literacy program if it provided services to your clients? Why or why not?

    _____

    _____

    _____

    Thank you for taking the time to help us by filling out this questionnaire.

NOTES

1. The State of Literacy in America: Estimates at the Local State and National Levels. 1998. Washington, D.C.: National Institute for Literacy.
2. Andy Hartman, Director, National Institute for Literacy, 800 Connecticut Avenue, NW, Suite 200, Washington, D.C. 20006-2712.

5 HOW DO YOU START?

> At Riverside City/County Library a family literacy learner/
> parent attended a City Council budget hearing. He explained
> that when his daughter was born he knew he had to do some-
> thing about his reading so that he could read to her and en-
> courage her education. He entered the library's program and
> three years later was preparing to enroll at Pepperdine Uni-
> versity. The City Council was very impressed with this new
> reader and his advancements as learner, worker, family mem-
> ber and citizen.
> —Randy Weaver, former literacy coordinator,
> Riverside City/County Library (Calif.)

DEVELOPING YOUR FAMILY LITERACY PROGRAM

Once you have assessed both the available resources and the existing needs in your community, you can begin to develop your family literacy program plan. Although it is important that all four of the basic components as defined in Chapter 1 (literacy for the adult, emerging literacy for children, interactive/intergenerational literacy, and parenting) are present, it is not always necessary, and sometimes is not feasible, for the library to be the sole provider of all the components.

When the California legislature developed plans in 1986 for the Families for Literacy program, which funds public libraries with the mandate that they provide all four components, it specified that in order to be eligible for funding, a library must already have established a successful adult literacy program. The lawmakers believed that for a library to begin all four components at the same time might be costly and very staff intensive. However, by extending services of an already existing library-based *adult* literacy program to the entire family, family literacy services could be efficiently and effectively provided at a reasonable cost.

The following are suggested steps in developing a family literacy program. At the end of this chapter are two sample program plans including community and program descriptions, staffing and budgets. One is typical of the plan a library might develop if it is providing all four components. The second plan follows the same goals and objectives but uses a budget where the library is a partner but not the sole provider of the family literacy program. Both are given here merely as examples and are not meant to be models to follow rigidly.

CREATING YOUR FAMILY LITERACY PROGRAM STEP BY STEP

STEP 1. DECIDE WHETHER THE LIBRARY WILL PROVIDE ALL FOUR OF THE BASIC COMPONENTS OF FAMILY LITERACY: adult literacy; emerging literacy for the children; programs and opportunities for intergenerational literacy activities for the family; and parenting discussions and information.

Some libraries find that the adult literacy component is costly and difficult for them to provide, even with volunteer tutors. If such is the case in your library, partnerships with local adult schools, community colleges, or community-based adult literacy programs may be set up so that these groups provide the adult component. Through your community-needs assessment (Chapter 4) you will have identified these other literacy providers and potential partners.

If you choose not to provide the adult literacy component within your own library, however, it is critical that you establish close and frequent communications with the agency or group that provides that component. When your staff is not providing the training for the adult's tutor or monitoring the teacher in the adult's literacy class, it is more difficult to systematically reinforce the importance of family literacy, especially intergenerational activities and parenting concerns. Frequent and positive communication with the trainers, tutors, and teachers is necessary if you want to have the optimum impact on the family. This is easier to establish and control when you provide the adult literacy component, but it can be done effectively through your partners if you have patience, persistence, and genuine buy-in and trust from your partner.

If your library staff is uncomfortable with providing the parenting component of family literacy, there are often health-affiliated and social service agencies that will be glad to provide this. A local college or university may have staff and student assistants/aides within their counseling, education, or social services departments who would be interested in taking on this component. Some programs have found a local professional counselor who is willing to partner with the program as a way of providing a community service.

Don't be afraid of the parenting component. When FFL first began, many of the children's librarians closely involved with the program were uneasy about addressing parenting issues. "I am a librarian, not a parenting expert or counselor," was a comment often heard. "How can I tell someone else how to be a parent when I have no real parenting experience myself?" asked others.

In response to these concerns, Jane Curtis, who had written the F.A.T.H.E.R.S. curriculum for the San Quentin project, and this author developed a curriculum that uses children's books to facilitate discussions and decision making about parenting issues and is based on the experiences in California. The curriculum is called P.A.R.E.N.T.S. for Parental Adults: Reading, Encouraging, Nurturing, Teaching, Supporting and was based upon many of the same premises already tested through the F.A.T.H.E.R.S. program.

The P.A.R.E.N.T.S. curriculum was field-tested for nearly two years in different family literacy settings (public libraries, jails, Even Start, shelters for abused women, teen-mom classes) in California and Hawaii and has proven highly successful and effective with both staff and adult learners. Some of the children's librarians who were most concerned initially about providing this service for FFL now find the parenting component one of the most interesting and rewarding activities.

Oakland's FFL coordinator, Judy Zollman, in an unpublished report wrote that the P.A.R.E.N.T.S. curriculum has been very successful. Participants have given positive feedback and willingly share information and experiences with other students. "We have seen an increase in students' confidence, parenting skills, and courage in sharing their failures and successes with other FFL parents." By taking advantage of the broad range of services provided by the library such as this component, "the scope of their learning is broadened."

A sample lesson from the *P.A.R.E.N.T.S. Curriculum Guide* is found in Appendix A. The guide was published by the California State Library Foundation and can be purchased by contacting them at (916) 447–6331 or writing to California State Library Foundation, 1225 8th Street, Suite 345, Sacramento, CA 95814.

STEP 2. FORM YOUR COLLABORATION.

Even if the library plans to provide all four components, community partners will be very valuable to you as you seek to recruit your families, gain visibility and support for your program, and develop additional resources. Plan to formalize your partnership; there should be written agreements among the partners that identify who will provide what for the partnership. Chapter 6 contains more information about collaborations.

STEP 3. REMEMBER TO INCLUDE POTENTIAL MEMBERS OF YOUR TARGET AUDIENCE SO THAT YOU CAN HAVE THEIR INPUT AND INSIGHT FROM THE BEGINNING.

In order to develop a successful program. you must have client buy-in; involving the client in the decision making is one critical way of achieving this.

One way of including adult learners in your program from the beginning is to invite them to participate as a focus group in your community needs assessment. If you are clear about the purposes for the group and why you are asking for their input, adult learners will be willing to participate because they are concerned about the welfare of their children. Even at San Quentin, where male inmates are often hardened and have given up on their own lives, inmates nearly always express a desire to have something better for their children. They often do not know that they can play an active role in making this happen, but they are willing to help and support a program that will benefit the children in their lives.

Seek out key community members in those communities in which many adult learners live. Ask them to help find those who will be willing to participate. Ask staff from your community partners, especially social workers and teachers, for names of potential participants whom they know or work with. Ministers and other religious leaders are often able to help find adults with low literacy who would work with you. If your library has an adult literacy program already, start with the adults who are enrolled. Your volunteer tutors can help you identify learners who might participate.

You may be surprised how many leaders emerge from the adult learners who serve on your Needs Assessment focus group or participate in your program collaboration. With training and support, they can not only provide valuable input to program planning and execution, they can become your most effective spokespersons and advocates. Many local communities now have adult learner organizations that are very active. A national organization of adult learners has also been formed which may be of help. It is called VALUE (Voice for Adult Literacy United for Education). You can find information on the Internet about this group at literacynet.org\value.

STEP 4. SET GOALS FOR YOUR PROGRAM WITH YOUR LIBRARY TEAM, REPRESENTATIVE POTENTIAL LEARNERS, AND YOUR COMMUNITY PARTNERS.

Based on the goals on information you gathered with the community literacy needs assessment, make your goals reflect your target audience as well as your community and library. You will probably want to define at least one goal for each of the four basic components of a full family literacy program.

Establish clear, measurable, and attainable objectives based on your goals. These should be consistent with your needs and resources. Plan now how you will evaluate your program. Remember it is usually better to do a limited number of things very well than to try to do so much for so many that nothing is done well.

Examples of goals and objectives for each component might include:

Adult literacy goal: Adults with preschool children in Roseville will become more literate.

Objectives:
1. Adults with preschool children will receive literacy tutoring.
2. At least 20 volunteer tutors will be trained to tutor adults in Roseville.
3. Tutoring will be provided twice each week for 1.5–2 hours at the library.
4. At least 15 adult learners will receive nine months of tutoring.
5. At least 15 adult learners will improve their literacy by one level based on pre and post scores as measured by the TABE (Test of Adult Basic Education).

Emerging literacy goal for children: Preschool children of adult literacy students in Roseville will enter school better prepared for reading and writing.

Objectives:
1. Preschool children of at least 20 adults receiving literacy tutoring will receive services to enhance and encourage their emerging literacy.
2. Special activities and opportunities for eligible children will be provided at least once per week at the library during the adult's tutoring sessions
3. At least 50 percent of children whose parents are being tutored will attend each session.
4. Activities will be fun and include, but not be limited to, songs, fingerplays, read-alouds, language-enhancing games, counting and numeracy activities, and other kindergarten readiness activities.

Interactive/intergenerational literacy goal: Roseville adult learners and their preschool children will engage each other in literacy activities.

Objectives:
1. At least 15 minutes of the adult learner's literacy sessions at least once each week will be spent working with his/her children learning and practicing activities that enhance and promote literacy.
2. Staff will model how to read aloud to children during each session

3. At least 80 percent of the adult learners will choose books to take home to practice this skill with their children.
4. At least 80 percent of the adult learners will keep monthly calendars of books read with their children.
5. At least 80 percent of adult learners will read to their children at least twice each week
6. At least 70 percent of the adult learners will show positive changes in their literacy activities at home with their children during a nine-month period as measured on the Family Literacy Parent Survey (Appendix H).

Parenting development goal: Adult learners in Roseville will know more about parenting and have more options in their parenting decision making.

Objectives:
1. At least once each month special parenting sessions will be held at the library for adult learners in the family literacy program.
2. Using children's books to facilitate discussions on parenting topics, adults will be introduced to some of the basic parenting issues.
3. At least 70 percent of the adult learners will attend at least 50 percent of the parenting sessions.
4. At least 70 percent of the adults who attend will report at the end of the nine months that they are satisfied or very satisfied with the parenting sessions.
5. At least 70 percent of the adults who attend will report at the end of the nine months that they feel better equipped to deal with parenting issues in their own lives.

STEP 5. DEVELOP YOUR BUDGET AND A TIME LINE.

The amount of money available may determine the number of families you plan to serve. Be realistic and specific. Include real dollars or in-kind support for staff salaries and benefits, materials, and general operations such as phone, postage, refreshments, incentives, and so on.

A time line is your "to do" list. It is a series of actions such as conducting a needs assessment, developing your collaboration, advertising for and hiring staff, and selecting and purchasing materials. Be realistic about your time. Things nearly always take longer to accomplish than anticipated.

Decide if you want a year-round program or one that operates for a few weeks or a few months. Some programs find that providing a series of activities once per week for a specific number of weeks (for example, six weeks or eight weeks) works better than once per month year round. Families may be better able to remember when to attend weekly programs, and the staff get breaks at the end of each series to plan and restructure if things need to be changed. Other communities like the once-per-month series of special programming, especially if certain times of the year (crop planting or picking season for farm workers) make it difficult for the families to participate during those months.

Through your community collaborations and the restructuring of priorities it is possible to create a viable family literacy program with little or no additional money. With partners who already provide needed services, you may be able to develop a program with no new funds by setting new priorities and working together to see that each component is provided by someone in a collaborative manner.

Even incentives can sometimes be acquired for free. Restaurants and local fast food stores may provide food for some of the activities or coupons for free food or discounts at their stores. Local organizations, especially Rotary, Soroptomist, Kiwanis, Altrusa, AAUW, and women's clubs, are often eager to purchase the children's books for your program. Because incentives such as giveaway books and food are crucial to the recruitment and retention of families in programs, it is important to budget for incentives from the beginning in case additional resources for these do not become available.

STEP 6. DEVELOP A STAFFING PLAN BASED ON YOUR BUDGET AND THE COMMITMENT OF THE VARIOUS PARTNERS.

Carefully define who is responsible for what, how often, when, and where. If no new staff are to be added, make sure the responsibilities are spread across all the partners and do not fall solely on just one member or agency in the collaboration.

STEP 7. DECIDE ON YOUR RECRUITMENT PLAN.

Enlist the help of your library staff, your community partners, potential clients, your volunteers, and anyone else in the community who will support your program. Chapter 7 provides specific suggestions for recruitment.

STEP 8. DEVELOP A CALENDAR FOR YOUR PROGRAM, A YEAR AT A TIME IF POSSIBLE.

Include events; special family programs in the library; tutor/teacher trainings, in-service programs, and support sessions; reports to the library or other funding sources; and regular meetings of the collaborating partners. Be realistic about what is doable given your staff and available resources.

Especially in the first year, less may be better. Do not plan too many events or schedule special programs too often. As your family literacy program evolves over time, additional opportunities can always be added.

STEP 9. PROVIDE ORIENTATION FOR ALL INVOLVED.

Inform library staff about the program and what to expect. Train volunteers/tutors/teachers in the basic concepts of family literacy and of your program. Tell the adult learners what to expect in this program and why. If special literacy staff are hired, make sure that good communication is established and maintained with the existing library staff. This is especially critical if the literacy program is to be housed outside of the library itself. The better prepared everyone is, the more successful will be the outcomes.

STEP 10. ACCESS AND USE THE MANY RESOURCES AVAILABLE ON THE INTERNET.

Numerous agencies and organizations have Web sites with valuable information about literacy and family literacy. Many of them have links to other sites that contain important information for parents and for programs.

Some of the more relevant sites are: the National Institute for Literacy (www.nifl.gov), the National Center for Family Literacy (www.famlit.org), the National Parent Information Network run by ERIC (www.npin.org), Yahoo's information about early childhood development and resources for parents and care-givers (www.iamyour child.org), and the Alliance for Childen and Families (alliance1.org). This list is far from complete and new sites are constantly being added.

STEP 11. BEGIN YOUR PROGRAM WITH A GREAT DEAL OF ENTHUSIASM AND COMMITMENT.

Be realistic about the amount of time it will take to create a full family literacy program. Many of California's most successful family literacy programs took two, three, and sometimes four years to develop completely. And, they are constantly changing to meet the needs of their changing populations.

Do not be discouraged if your community does not immediately adopt your new program as a valued service. The results of family literacy are long term, and the successful implementation can take many years, especially when you have little or no funding.

Cathy Clady, formerly family literacy coordinator for San Diego Public Library, related how hard it can sometimes be to get started.

If first sessions set the stage for future sessions, we (Valencia Park Branch of San Diego Public Library) would have elected to return all the [FFL] monies and withdraw from future consideration.

After much planning and anticipation we were ready to open our first session when God decided to water the lawn the night before the program. Unfortunately, we had just finished a major landscaping the night before the rain. Our roots hadn't taken. Top soil, decorative rocks and all, flowed into the building, flooding out the main portion of the library.

Rain and flood, we still had 17 families show up for their first session. Undaunted, we cleared the dark and damp garage and held our first session amid crying babies and cheering parents. At that moment we know we had something special these families wanted—books, books, and more books.

Children were attached to their parents, didn't respond to storytime, refused to separate into breakout groups, and cried for hours on end. However, after two months, the children were eager, receptive, and highly auditory. Parents had to coax these same introverts to quiet down and coerce them to leave. Parents were so enthused about the parenting sessions that presenters were often mobbed with questions. Parents even followed the presenters out to the parking lot thanking them for their help and information. I'm so glad we persisted and did not get discouraged based on our first experiences (unpublished internal report).

HOW TO ADDRESS THE FOUR BASIC COMPONENTS OF FAMILY LITERACY

Adult literacy: Ideally your library is already providing or willing to provide the adult literacy component. However, if your library does not provide adult literacy services and is not interested in beginning this component, you may partner with another agency or group that does.

A good way to begin is with learners already enrolled in an adult literacy program. If you target families of adults in Adult Basic Education (ABE) or English as a Second Language (ESL) classes, be sure that the teacher/administrator/school is brought into the idea of family literacy so that he/she can reinforce the concepts during the classes. Train volunteer tutors to support family literacy in their literacy sessions with the adults and teach them to value and promote the family as the center for literacy activities of all kinds.

Emerging literacy for children: Most libraries already provide many types of programming to support the emerging literacy needs of children. They are very good at designing storytimes, puppet shows, and other activities that are both entertaining and educational. The children who typically attend these programs, however, are those whose parents already value reading and understand the importance of these early literacy activities for their children.

The children most at risk of not becoming literate are those who do not attend the special offerings of the library. One of the major objectives of most library-based family literacy programs is to bring these children into the library for special family literacy activities and eventually mainstream them into regular children's programming.

The special programming that you offer can take many forms. Sometimes you will find that offering a special event each month, often in conjunction with a holiday or season or special theme, works very well. Others have found that trying to get families to remember a date once every month is difficult and takes too many reminders. They find that scheduling programming once each week for a series of weeks works better. Some families seem to be able to commit more easily to this type of schedule, knowing that they will be off for a month or more at the conclusion. In this structure the families are usually anxious for the new series to begin. Each community is different. Your will have to find out what works best for yours.

Lynda Nield, the adult and family literacy coordinator at Woodland (Calif.) Public Library, described a typical program in her library in their 1997/98 FFL Final Report.

FFL meetings are held in five consecutive Wednesday evenings from 5:30–7:00 pm The first 30 minutes is a social time where everyone comes together (parents, children, tutors, volunteers, and staff) and there is food, usually a meal. From 6:00–6:40 everyone is separated into individual teams, parent(s) with the individual tutor and children in age groups of preschool age 2–5 years, 5–8 years, and 8 years and older. With the preschoolers there are always two to three volunteers who provide music, singing, arts, crafts, and reading activities. Tutors and parents go over the new books to be given to the children that night. The tutors have been trained with the interactive dialogue method of presenting books and demonstrate to the parents how to utilize this method of interacting and sharing books with their children. Weekly book charts are completed by parents and tutors if not already done at home by the parents. Any other materials or information for the parents to help them with their child's reading and preparation for school is also presented at this time, such as how to make the home a learning lab and other activities parents might do with their children. Older siblings are given reading, art, and writing activities along with homework help. Many times the older siblings assist their younger siblings in the preschool activities. We have found that the "older" participants in our program have been very positive additions to the program and provide marvelous "role" models for all of the younger children. Then from 6:40–7:00 the entire group comes back together for storytime and related games, songs and other activities (unpublished internal report).

When California's FFL program first began, one concern often voiced by the children's librarians who worked with family programs was their lack of knowledge about how to develop intergenerational activities and storytimes that would appeal to diverse age groups as found in literacy families. All of these librarians soon realized that the adults and children were so eager for these opportunities that it was easy for the books and newness of the materials to bridge the age gap. Indeed, it was sometimes the parents and older siblings who were so enthralled that they did not want to leave a session when it was over. The children's librarians did not have to develop new programs. They were often able to modify their existing programs and storytimes to the family setting.

Family literacy programs must also be sure that the tutor or teacher is constantly modeling and reinforcing what the adults need to do to support their children's emerging literacy. This could include such things as reading aloud, duet reading, expanding and developing on stories read, telling family stories, and writing and illustrating family "books." Never lose sight of the role the parent plays as the first and most important child's teacher. Special programming in the library is only one way to support this critical component, not the *only* way.

Tutors and/or teachers are key to success in providing emerging literacy for children. If the adult's tutoring session is an hour long, at least 15 minutes in every lesson should be devoted to supporting the adult learner in meeting the literacy needs of his/her children. In a classroom setting, at least two half-hour lessons each week should be designed to help adults develop skills and techniques with which to help their children.

Tutors and teachers must remind adult learners to take every opportunity possible to model the use and value of reading and writing at home, on the bus, or in the car—wherever they go. These activities in turn reinforce and extend the adult's own literacy skills.

Intergenerational Activities: Many of the activities in which libraries already engage children can become intergenerational when the adult is invited and encouraged to participate. Adults and even older siblings who have not been read to as young children generally find storytimes and activities meant for younger children very exciting. It is not unusual to find them more engrossed and attentive than the younger siblings who are not yet used to sitting still and listening to books or watching a puppet show. For many, this is their first introduction to the colorful, fun, and exciting world of children's literature.

Many preliteracy or emerging literacy skills can be effectively taught to children by low-literate adults. Wordless picture books can be used to demonstrate how to hold a book, turn pages, and interact with the pictures without relying on text. Interactive books such as the I Spy series of children's books or *Andy's Pirate Ship* can be used to practice and improve visual discrimination skills. *The Very Hungry Caterpillar* not only teaches basic left-to-right progression but sequencing, colors, numbers, names of fruits and days of the week, as well as many other basic concepts. Children's books teach without being overtly "teachy."

Cooking is one example of a fun, family activity and using cookbooks can provide literacy practice. Coloring, drawing, and crafts are also great activities. Parents are often surprised and impressed with the skills and talents their children show during these times. Most children's librarians have many resources already at their disposal in which to find ideas for intergenerational activities. And, don't forget to make reading aloud intergenerational, too! Tutors and teachers should read aloud to adult learners; adult learners read aloud to their children and their tutors or teachers; and children, as soon as they are able, should read aloud to adults.

Parenting: Most libraries already have books on parenting on their shelves. Many, if not all of these, however, will be at too high a reading level for the average adult learner. You should probably begin by purchasing a few, easy-to-read books on parenting and making these available to adults and tutors. Some suggestions are contained in the bibliography of easy-to-read parenting materials in Appendix B.

Interactive discussions are a great way to tackle parenting issues. Chapter 8 provides many specific ideas for addressing parenting concerns.

TWO MODELS OF FAMILY LITERACY PROGRAMS

Even though there is not just one right way to do family literacy, nor one perfect model of how a family literacy program should look, it may still be helpful to briefly describe two different successful models that can be found in many libraries. Rose Library demonstrates a model in which the library provides all services with support from community partners. Knox Library is one in which the library is an important partner but not the sole provider of services.

ROSE LIBRARY'S FAMILY LITERACY WITH FUN AND FLAIR (FLFF)

Rose Library serves a community of approximately 40,000 people. Although this library has its own adult literacy program, they work closely with the local elementary school to help recruit families identified as having limited literacy materials and activities in the home. These two partners began meeting and talking about providing family literacy for their community for four months before they actually instituted a full program. A thorough needs assessment identified a clear need for a family literacy program in Roseville.

Elementary teachers send home information about FLFF and encourage families to get involved. Volunteer tutors from the library literacy program call families identified by the teachers as "at risk" and invite them individually to attend FLFF activities. Written invitations are also sent out addressed to the individual children, inviting them to the FLFF "parties" at the library. It is very difficult for an adult not to respond when their children become excited about the prospect of attending a party they have been invited to!

Roseville is an ethnically diverse community with approximately 49 percent white, 30 percent Latino, 12 percent African American, 8 percent Asian and 1 percent Pacific Islander or Native American. Adults enrolling in the library's literacy program are reasonably representative of this ethnic mix. The family literacy program is made up of 55 percent Latino families, 25 percent white families, 10 percent African American families, 4 percent Asian families and 1 percent Native American families. In order to best reflect this diversity, every effort is made to include staff from various ethnic groups in the programs.

Monthly parties are held September through May at the library for these families exclusively. They are not much different from traditional storytimes except for their titles and the fact that they address the whole family. These parties generally last about one to one and one-half hours since many of the children are too young to enjoy much more than that. Each "party" consists of reading aloud from three to five books in addition to other activities.

These parties are generally held when the library is closed so that the families can use the entire library for such activities as library scavenger hunts without disturbing other patrons. Adults unaccustomed to the library are always concerned about their children being too noisy or too active and this helps to alleviate some of that concern.

These parties always have a theme, and the books, refreshments, and other activities are built around that theme. Food is generally served first to help ensure that the families will arrive on time. Sometimes the food is a snack, sometimes a full meal donated by a local service club or restaurant, and sometimes the families contribute pot

At Blanchard Community Library (Santa Paula, CA) children in the family literacy program increase their literacy readiness through experiences such as visiting a local farm.

luck dishes to accompany a main entree that is provided or donated. Because it is a community of great diversity, the family literacy program uses activities, books, and themes that reflect this diversity, introducing the families to stories and culture of their own ethnic groups as well as other groups.

A typical party progresses from food to an action song or activity that loosens everyone up and creates a setting of fun and closeness. This is followed by a storytime featuring stories from various children's books expanded and extended through the use of puppets, flannel boards, fingerplays, songs, and such. These are almost always done by a children's librarian with the same materials she/he uses in regular children's programming. One major difference is that the librarian knows that these parents need to have more explanation and information about *why* to do certain things as well as *how* to do them. It is also important to help the FLFF parents see the ways that their children can be engaged and involved in all these activities that enhance literacy development.

Next, the children and parents have a related craft or art activity demonstrated for them; then they work on this together. Sometimes during this part of the program, the parents move to another, nearby room and discuss parenting topics such as health, nutrition, discipline, or sibling rivalry. When the adults are having facilitated discussions, the children are helped with their activities by a local Girl Scout troop. (An added bonus is that the Scouts clean up the activity afterwards— particularly helpful when carving pumpkins or making gingerbread houses!)

At the end of the party each child is invited to choose a gift book to take home. Often the children will want to choose one of the books that was read that evening. A large collection of varying age and topic interest is kept for this purpose. If a program does not have enough giveaway books for each child, then one per family may be chosen. In addition, Rose Library's FLFF keeps a calendar of the program children's birthdays and sends a birthday card to each child with an invitation to come into the library and receive a specially selected gift book from the children's librarian (see Figure 5.1 for sample budget). This encourages the family to come to the library on its own during regular library hours and gives the children's librarian an opportunity to show the family around on a private tour.

Family literacy is supported by the individual volunteer tutors who tutor the adults in these families. All tutors receive special training in the what, why, and how of family literacy. They not only encourage their learners to attend but follow up in their next tutoring sessions with activities that support the entire family. Tutors are also encouraged to attend the monthly parties, and some even bring their adult learners and families with them.

Figure 5.1 Rose Library Family Literacy Budget

Item	Cost	Source
Children's Librarian (attends 9 parties or programs per year + planning/collaboration meetings)	.10 FTE	in-kind from library
FLFF Coordinator	.25 FTE	volunteer
Training of tutors	.10 FTE	in-kind from literacy program
Food/refreshments		donated
Craft & art supplies	$900	($100 per party)
Gift books	$2,000	($50 per family X 40 families)
Other incentives	$200	
TOTAL	$3,100	Mostly from local donations

In addition to monthly parties and regular tutoring sessions, special workshops for tutors and learners are held every eight to ten weeks. These workshops are stand-alone, three-hour workshops that also enhance and expand the tutoring experience. Learners and tutors both suggest topics for the workshops. Sessions on spelling, grammar, writing, and phonics are popular. These workshops are well attended and meaningful childcare is offered for the children of attending tutors and learners. Workshops are presented by staff and/or volunteers from the adult literacy program, teachers from the local school, retired teachers from the local council of the International Reading Association, or sometimes by the learners themselves.

KNOX PUBLIC LIBRARY

Knox Library serves a community of over 100,000 people. The library does not have its own adult literacy program but was concerned that the students from the local adult school and the parents of the Head Start children did not bring their children to the library or participate in any of the programming activities of their children's services division.

The Friends of the Library conducted a community needs assessment. They found that although the Head Start program had some monies dedicated to family literacy, there was not a mechanism anywhere in the community to bring together those adults and their children who were at risk of continuing the cycle of low literacy or illiteracy to promote family literacy activities and involvement.

A special family literacy committee from the Friends convinced the principal of the adult school and the director of the local Head Start to meet monthly with the librarian in charge of children's services for nearly one year to carefully plan, organize, and implement a family literacy program. Each agency signed a written agreement to collaborate (see Chapter 6 for more information) on the project and each agreed to contribute to the project in-kind or actual dollars. As the planning progressed, other local partners were brought in (including the Soroptomist Club, the owner of the local Pizza Hut, a nearby bookstore specializing in children's books, the local newspaper, the PTA from the elementary school, and the local TARGET store).

Because of the size of the program, the planning committee knew that a paid coordinator would be necessary if the project were to succeed. Contributions from the library (training money) and Head Start (staff development money) were combined since the coordinator would be responsible for family literacy training for both of these groups. With additional donations from the Friends of the Library and the PTA, enough money was garnered to pay for a .75 FTE coordinator for the Knox Family Literacy Initiative (KFLI). Figure 5.2 shows the budget.

The first job for the KFLI coordinator once hired, was to train the adult school and Head Start teachers and children's services staff at the library in the basics of family literacy. Each group clearly identified the roles they could play in the overall project.

Adult school teachers would encourage adult students to participate in the KFLI programs, use children's books in the classroom for learning opportunities, and take their classes for special visits to the library and to get library cards. Those who got library cards and checked out books would get special credit.

Head Start teachers would recruit parents to both the adult school classes and the KFLI programs, transport families to the library for special programs, and see that the children got library cards. They would recruit Head Start parents to be trained as read-aloud partners for the Head Start children. They would also alert the librarian to any special topics or activities that they were using so that a collection of related library books could be brought to the center for display and a longer checkout.

Children's librarians agreed to: hold special programs one morning each month for the Head Start children and parent(s); train volunteer Head Start parents to read aloud to the children; introduce the services of the library to the adult classes; and conduct once each week for six weeks a series of family literacy programs for the KFLI families. This series would be given three times, once at the main library

Figure 5.2 Knox Public Library Family Literary Budget

Item	Cost		Source	
KFLI Coordinator	.75 FTE	$27,000	(Head Start	$6,000)
			(Library	6,000)
			(PTA	8,000)
			(Friends	7,000)
Children's Librarian (18 parties or programs per year + planning/collaboration meetings)	.25 FTE		in-kind library	
Food/refreshments			donated by Pizza Hut & others	
Craft & art supplies			donated by TARGET	
Gift books @ $50 per family x 80 families =		$4,000	($3,000 donated by local bookstore &Soroptomist + $1,000 raised locally)	
Other incentives		$1,000	$1,000 raised by local donations	
	Total	$32,000		

and once each at the two branch libraries closest to the communities identified as most at risk.

The special KFLI programs provided by the children's librarian were similar in makeup to those of the Rose Library. The day of the week and time of day offered differed, however, with the community. At Central Library, the KFLI programs were offered Thursday evenings from 7:00–8:30 p.m. At Horse Creek Branch the programs were held on Saturday mornings from 11:00 until the library opened at 12:30. Vista Branch found that Tuesday morning from 10:00 to noon worked best for their community. On those days, Head Start moms and their preschool children were brought to the library in the Head Start vans.

6 WHO PAYS FOR THE PROGRAM?

> I wasn't at all convinced at the beginning that literacy belonged in public libraries. But, what the heck, the grant was offered and I thought why not. Four years later I now see that adult and family literacy programs bring much more to the library than they cost the library. They bring community good will, new patrons, new partners and contributors, and a wonderful sense of accomplishment.
>
> —Ginny Cooper, former library director,
> Alameda County (Calif.) Library

FUNDING WHAT YOU FOUND

Even after many of the other challenges have been met, funding remains a critical issue for most libraries when developing a family literacy program. Indeed, lack of funding is probably the most commonly cited reason for a library's inability to provide family literacy as an ongoing service. It is important to understand, however, that not all family literacy programs require additional money.

Libraries can and do develop full family literacy projects without additional funding. They can prioritize differently so that existing staff time and funding is dedicated to the literacy effort. Certainly family literacy programs take staff time, but it is not always necessary to hire new staff or reorganize existing staff to free up a full-time position.

Many library-based family literacy programs are begun and managed by either part-time staff or by the children's librarian, a adult literacy staff person, or both, who makes family literacy a priority for the library. If your library has doubts about why they need to provide family literacy, just refer them to your own library's Mission Statement! (See Chapter 3 for more information.)

It is also possible to develop a full family literacy program by collaborating with other agencies in such a manner that each provides services already available in their programs, but focuses these on a specific, mutually agreed upon target audience in a collaborative manner.

It is not always necessary for the library to provide all the component services; instead, one may choose to work with various partners to ensure that all components are addressed. More information about partnerships in family literacy and guidelines concerning community collaborations are found later in this chapter.

WHERE ARE THE DOLLARS?

Believe it or not, libraries that take on family literacy as a regular service of the library can benefit financially. Benefactors who have never before donated to a library are often attracted to literacy and to the idea of supporting a "family effort." Companies and businesses that have never given to a publicly supported institution ("You must have that 501(c)3 or we can't contribute!") want to give their philanthropic dollars to a program that enhances children and families. Family literacy as a philanthropy is attractive to many companies, foundations, civic or professional groups, and individuals because of the holistic, family approach it takes to solving a problem that ultimately affects all of us.

There is also government support for these needed programs. The Library Services Program, Title I of the Library Services and Construction Act (LSCA), has been around since the early 1970s. In the 1984 reauthorization of LSCA, Congress increased the emphasis on literacy, making it a separate priority under Title I and adding Title VI, a new literacy component, to the act. Even though the funding allotted to Title VI grew steadily and President Clinton stated that he was very committed to the continuation of this, Title VI was eliminated in 1996.

Federal funding for library programs (including literacy) is now allocated as Library Services and Technology Act (LSTA) and final decisions about which projects of what type are funded reside within each state library. LSTA Title I, however, can be used to fund family literacy programs.

Although the National Center for Family Literacy (NCFL) does not award funding to family literacy programs, it does provide assistance. Its publication, *Funding a Family Literacy Program*, contains helpful tips and suggestions and is available from NCFL by calling 512–584–1133 and asking for publications. In addition, NCFL usually conducts a number of workshops on fund-raising at their annual spring conference in Louisville, Kentucky.

FEDERAL LITERACY GRANTS

The 1998 Adult Education and Family Literacy Act for the first time designates family literacy programs as eligible for these federal funds. This act defines family literacy services as "services that are of sufficient intensity in terms of hours, and of sufficient duration, to make sustainable changes in a family, and that integrate all of the following activities . . . " It then proceeds to list the four basic components of family literacy as given throughout this book. Libraries are also identified as eligible agencies to receive such funds.

Although available to libraries for family literacy programs, these funds may prove hard to access. Many of the required activities and performance accountability measures will be beyond the scope of what libraries wish to address. Core indicators of performance, however, have been broadened from just demonstration of literacy skills to encompass a much wider spectrum, including completion of training, postsecondary education, or unsubsidized employment or career advancement. This broadening may be beneficial to libraries seeking funding under the act.

Even Start

Even Start began as a federally funded family literacy program in 1989. When the national allocation of dollars grew beyond a specified amount, Even Start funds became block grants to the states in 1992. These programs are now administered locally by each state's department of education.

Even Start is aimed at families in which one or both parents need basic skills education and have at least one child from birth through age seven. The child must also reside in a Chapter 1 participating attendance area.

During its first four years, Even Start delivered family literacy services to more than 20,000 families at a federal cost of about $2,500 per family per year. However, the average adult in Even Start programs entered with the literacy skills of a high school student as measured by the reading scale of CASAS (Comprehensive Adult Student Assessment System.). Generally these were not, therefore, the hard to reach and serve adults with literacy skills below sixth grade level.

Each month the typical Even Start family received an average of 13.5 hours of adult education, 6.5 hours of parenting education, and 26 hours of early childhood education. This data is available on the Even Start home page on the World Wide Web. At the time of publication, this and other information about this program could be accessed at their site at www.ed.gov/pubs/Biennial/104.html.

Even Start provides funding for four years of programs that address the four basic components of family literacy. Public and school libraries have often been included in Even Start grants as collaborating partners, but few libraries have been the lead recipients. In California at least two public libraries have applied for Even Start grants, but as of 1998, neither had been funded.

America Reads

America Reads Challenge is a broad initiative of President Clinton's administration, a challenge that President Clinton issued in his 1997 State of the Union Address. Its mission is to ensure that every child in

Children from Napa City/County Library's FFL program thank Starbucks for their gift books.

the United States is able to read independently by the end of the third grade. Although the final federal appropriation for FY 99 for this program was $260,000,000, most of this will go to elementary and secondary schools. Family literacy efforts are included and public libraries are eligible for these dollars but may find partnerships with local LEAs (Local Education Authorities) their most viable way to access these funds. For more information call 1-800-USA-LEARN.

FOUNDATIONS AND CORPORATIONS

A number of private and corporate foundations have a strong interest in either children or literacy. Some have already developed a focus specifically on family literacy. For the best known ones, however, the competition for the dollars is very stiff. The Barbara Bush Family Literacy Foundation, for instance (discussed in Chapter 1), funds a number of programs each year, primarily in urban areas, but always has many more applications than it can fund.

Coors, Coca-Cola, Wal-Mart, Pizza Hut, Target, GTE, Starbucks, Amazon.com and numerous other corporate sponsorships for family literacy are possible. However, many foundations will give only in certain geographic areas or only for projects serving specific groups.

Information about possible literacy funders is available on the World Wide Web. Regularly check the grants sections of such sites as those of the National Institute for Literacy and the National Center for Family Literacy. Most popular search engines will also help you search the Web widely for interested potential funders. In general, however, it may be easier for most libraries to look locally for support.

TIPS FOR ASKING FOR MONEY LOCALLY

Many local groups and individuals prefer to give donations to specific projects but do not like to fund ongoing staff or operational expenses. Some programs avoid reference to this by creating "Adopt a Family" campaigns.

- Using an "adoption" approach, companies, groups, and individuals can be told exactly how much they need to donate to provide services to support a family through the program. Full descriptions of the family, its needs, and its progress can be reported to the sponsor(s), but be sure not to use real names or information that would identify a specific family. Send the sponsors drawings and letters from the children as well as letters from the adults. These can be part of the literacy practice for the family while serving as very positive feedback for the sponsor. Your tutors can help with this. It is time consuming but can be very profitable.

- Many companies and businesses have programs in which they will match employee donations to organizations. Some will count volunteer time as part of the match. Remind your tutors and other literacy volunteers to find out if their employers have such programs and if they do, the volunteer should apply for them.

- Consider developing a Speaker's Bureau of trained volunteers who are effective motivational speakers (or can be trained to be good speakers) to go throughout the community promoting your program and soliciting funds. These speakers can be library staff, volunteer tutors, staff, or clients from your partner agencies, just to name a few. The most effective speakers are well-trained adult learners whose families have received services from your program. Just telling their own stories makes these beneficiaries of family literacy very credible speakers. Include the children when appropriate.

  Speakers should always be prepared to describe a very specific need and exactly how much it will cost. Donations for incentives for your program, especially for children's books, are always popular. Many people prefer donating to something that benefits children.

- Participate in well-known donation campaigns such as United Way. They will take a small percentage for overhead and promotions, but generally give most of the donations directly to the designated organization. Many large employers, such as some state governments, promote employee involvement in United Way and make it easier to get employees to contribute regularly to a specific program by having the donations deducted monthly from their salary checks.
- Encourage volunteers, patrons and staff to donate money to the program as memorials for family or friends. Publish this in your newsletters, local newspapers, and other places where appropriate.
- Keep a list of your donors and patrons and contact them yearly. When you do receive donations, always follow up with a thank you and a description of how the money will be used. Use photos of your families (with their permission) and literacy activities to personalize the thank you letters. Donors who know their contributions were used well, see tangible results and receive thanks are much more likely to contribute again!

Tips for Holding Fund-Raising Events

Fund-raising events on behalf of family literacy can be very exciting and profitable, but they also require much time and work.

- Sponsor book fairs, spelling bees, trivia bees, goods and services auctions or similar activities. These have all been used successfully by library programs. They might also raise the visibility of your program in the community.
- Be careful, however, that the event itself does not demand so much time from program staff that it takes too much away from the program. Only undertake a major fund-raising event when a cadre of volunteers, at least some of whom are experienced in such events, is at your disposal. Do not set up events so that program staff do all the work.

Tips for Getting Internal Funding

The ideal situation for most successful family literacy programs in the library is to have secure and stable base funding from your city or county and to only solicit additional funding for the "extras." This will be easier to do if you have involved your key governmental decision-makers in your program planning from the beginning.

- Be sure that local governmental officers and elected officials are apprised of the program and invited to your activities.
- Set up photo opportunities that promote your program in the media and use these to lure support from those who must seek votes.
- Cultivate state and federal legislators who represent your community also, for they may be able to help you.

COMMUNITY COLLABORATIONS AND PARTNERSHIPS

Many of the most successful family literacy programs are those that form cooperative partnerships with other groups in their communi-

Numerous community partners in the Inland area of Southern California work together to make their annual family literacy celebration a success. (Hans reads the stock quotes while waiting.)

ties. Participating groups, agencies, businesses, or organizations often include Head Start, Even Start, adult schools, colleges and universities, professional or business groups, labor, daycare providers, service clubs, social services, health providers, local bookstores, children's toy or clothing businesses, and pediatric groups.

For many communities, family literacy can be the catalyst for moving the library into the center of community activities. Some public library directors in California are convinced that it was their family literacy programs that finally made the local city council or county board of supervisors take notice of the library and appreciate its value to all the members of the community.

Family literacy can give the library new visibility and new value in a way traditional library services seldom do. It can help to enhance and develop the role of the library as the community center.

Collaboration is not, however, easy. It can take a great deal of time and energy to establish and maintain a collaboration that works. Even when very successful, collaborations may depend heavily upon particular individuals to sustain them. If one or more of these people leave or change positions, the remaining partners may not find the new person interested in continuing the partnership. At the very best, a good deal of time may be required just to bring the new person up to a level of understanding that will keep the partnership alive.

The value of collaboration does offset the price the library must pay in staff time. Multiagency partnerships provide not only for the cross-pollination of ideas, expertise, and resources, but also afford a level of visibility and respect in the community which is not otherwise possible. In addition, community members like to see their tax money being used efficiently and effectively by the leveraging and sharing of responsibilities and resources that take place in a collaboration.

Partnerships and collaborations cannot only bring valuable resources such as shared staff, meeting or office space, specific expertise, or numerous other contributions, but can also bring in actual dollars. An example of this is the exciting partnership formed in California among the Families for Literacy program, the California State Library Foundation, Wells Fargo Bank, and Huell Howser, author of the video series *California's Gold*.

HUELL HOWSER AND FFL

The very successful video series produced, written, and narrated by Mr. Howser was underwritten by Wells Fargo Bank. Wells Fargo wanted to make this series available to schools and educational institutions at a reasonable cost while at the same time providing royalties for Mr. Howser. Mr. Howser wanted to donate a portion of his proceeds of the sales to a related cause. The idea of using the money to purchase children's books for at-risk families in family literacy programs appealed to him.

The money is placed in an account with the California State Library Foundation and then distributed to each library with a Families for Literacy program. The amount each library receives is based on the number of families enrolled in its family literacy program. This money is used to buy children's books, which are given to the FFL families. Families and staff then write letters of appreciation and thanks to all concerned and describe what a difference the books and the programs have made. Everyone is happy and the partnership works!

In 1997 the FFL programs decided to thank Mr. Howser for his donations. Children, parents, and staff in each program created a personalized fabric square. These were sewn together and hand quilted, making a large wall hanging. A group of children from some of the FFL programs then presented the quilt to Mr. Howser at the annual meeting of the California Library Association. He was so surprised and moved that he could barely speak. The quilt became a wonderful thank you, brought attention from the library community to the FFL programs, and helped to ensure that the partnership will continue.

Family literacy also appeals to a broad sector of the community. Civic and professional groups such as Rotary, Soroptomist, Kiwanis, Lions, and Altrusa often sponsor all or portions of family literacy programs.

FAMTRACK

FAMTRACK, a family literacy program piloted for two years in five California public libraries, used a family meal as well as literacy as the focus for bringing families into the library. In a number of these communities, local groups like Soroptomist provided and served meals for the family meetings. In some of the FAMTRACK communities restaurants and grocers provided free food for these meals as well as free meal certificates to be used as incentives for the families who participated in the program.

PASADENA PUBLIC LIBRARY

Pasadena Public Library found that its Families for Literacy program was so successful and popular that the local Rotary Club offered to purchase all of the children's books used to give away to the families. An attractive bookplate was designed with space for the name of the child and a notation that the book is a gift from the Pasadena Rotary Club and the Pasadena Public Library.

NATIONAL CITY PUBLIC LIBRARY

National City Public Library developed a partnership with San Diego

State University. They worked with 14 teacher-training undergraduates who participated in a course titled "Family Literacy Outreach" in which they worked with "high risk" families in their homes.

In order to recruit the families and set a positive atmosphere for working together, the library staff designed a special recruitment pitch that made the families themselves active, contributing partners in the university class. The families were asked to assist the university in providing a rich learning experience for young, teachers-in-training. In essence, the families would be opening up their home for the benefit of the teacher interns. In turn, the families would benefit from the special information and tutoring that the students could offer. The families also each received seven free gift books for their preschool children.

The approach worked very well in securing the cooperation of the families in a manner that left them feeling like they were not guinea pigs or "people with deficits," but rather full partners in a mutually beneficial activity. Comments from the future teachers indicated that they benefited as much from the partnership as did the families. The program was so successful in 1994 that it was repeated in 1995.

GUIDELINES FOR SUCCESSFUL PARTNERSHIPS AND COLLABORATIONS

Partnerships lead to success. However, in order for any partnership to succeed over time, each partner must be a contributor as well as a receiver of benefit from the partnership. The partnership or collaboration must be a two-way street, with each committing resources in pursuit of a shared goal. It is helpful to take the time to understand the structure of each organization and be sure that each partner has top level approval for and understanding of the collaboration.

A common goal must be defined and written guidelines for the partnership established. When developing the partnership it may be advisable to formalize it by having a written Memorandum of Agreement. This should be signed by all parties, renewable yearly but cancelable with sufficient notice. A sample Memorandum of Agreement developed for a Library-Head Start- family literacy partnership is found in Appendix C.

Even loosely organized partnerships need some written guidelines. Most businesses that donate to programs require at the least a formal request on official letterhead stating what is being requested and how and for whom it will be used. It is also always advisable to thank the donor and provide a written description of how the donation contributed to the success of the program. Specific anecdotes enhance the thank you letters and notes. Letters, drawings, or crafts from the children or families can also contribute to the effectiveness of the response.

Schedule regular meetings of the partners. Have a well-organized agenda and move through it quickly. See that each partner has a role in the agenda and does not just sit passively listening to others. Provide ongoing positive feedback.

Generally libraries have a lot of support within their communities. Numerous other agencies and organizations share similar goals. You will identify many "natural" partners during your needs assessment. But, be cautious that the library isn't doing *all* the work. Because of the commitment of staff and the general service-oriented atmosphere found in most libraries, it is very easy to find yourself providing all the services instead of sharing the workload with your partners. This is not a true collaboration and you may soon find yourself overextended and burned out. Then no one benefits.

For more detailed information on collaborating for family literacy, see Quesada and Nickse's book *Community Collaborations for Family Literacy* (New York: Neal-Schuman, 1993).

SERVING SPECIAL POPULATIONS

Do not ignore the needs of the special populations in your community, such as those found in correctional facilities, homeless shelters, and rehabilitation sites. Partnering with the agencies that serve these groups can be very rewarding. Sometimes, especially with prison populations, there may be money available through inmate welfare funds or sheriff's funds to help support the effort. Often federal and state grants are available to help you serve these populations with special needs.

Special populations are difficult to serve because in addition to the array of problems and issues present with most low-literate families, these families have other, seemingly insurmountable issues with which to contend.

FAMILY LITERACY FOR THE INCARCERATED

Incarcerated individuals see their families seldom, if at all. When visitation does occur it can be very stressful and chaotic. Phone contact is usually less than satisfying, particularly with very young children.

Children whose parents are incarcerated often think that they are somehow to blame for their parents' absence or imprisonment. "If I had only been better, or smarter, maybe my mother/father/grandfather would not be in jail" is a common feeling.

Family literacy in a correctional setting can provide most of the same resources as any program on the outside, except for a high level of intergenerational interaction. These parents can come to view themselves as role models and accept this responsibility. They can learn positive ways of interacting with their children. They can assure their children that the child is not to blame for what happened to the parent.

If parents have visitation with the child, they can use these times more positively by listening to and reading with the child. Visitation times in most correctional settings are noisy and chaotic. Children must compete with each other and with the other parent for time with the incarcerated adult. Distractions and interruptions abound. However, many of these annoyances can be overcome if the adult will sit with the child(ren) holding a book and reading aloud quietly. This positive experience in an otherwise negative environment allows for familial bonding as well as positive interaction around a good book.

If they do not have visitation, incarcerated adults can record themselves reading a book aloud. The child can then be given that book by the program or can find it at the library. The child then listens to the parent reading on the tape while looking at the book at home. In some settings, however, security regulations may not allow recorded tapes to be sent or mailed home.

A number of libraries have successfully provided adult or family literacy services to local jails and prisons. Some successful model programs in California can be found at Santa Clara County Free Library, Alameda County Library, Ventura County Library, and Siskiyou County. Former Director of Siskiyou County's Read Project Jeannette McCarroll described her jail program in a recent FFL report:

> Our continuing relationship with the county jail has provided us with a wonderful way for inmates to impart positive reading attitudes and habits to their children. The Read to Me Program (FFL program in the jail) has been beneficial to our library and to the jail. We receive program referrals from inmates and by participating in the jail program they are able to do something positive for themselves and their families. Jail personnel have noted the positive influence of this program upon participating inmates (unpublished internal report).

The first step in successfully working with incarcerated adults is to work with the custody officers to win their support and approval. If custody can be convinced that your program will make their jobs easier, they will usually agree to partner with you. Start at the top and work your way down the staff hierarchy. Make friends of the officers on the wing or floor. Never forget that security is their first concern and anything that may threaten it will be difficult for them to support.

Recognize and plan for the likelihood that some of the children's books and materials used with this population will disappear. It is difficult, if not impossible, to keep careful watch on materials used in a correctional setting. In the program at San Quentin State Prison, children's books used during visitation times were kept in a locked cabinet to which only custody had a key. About four months into the program a children's librarian arrived to provide a storytime one Saturday morning only to find all the books had disappeared. The books were never found, but I am confident that some child in some home is using those books. We purchased another set and resumed our programs.

Inmates have much time to think about their roles as parents or caregivers. They truly are a "captive" audience for your programs. Most of them want something better for their children than they have experienced for themselves. Family literacy provides information and direction to accomplishing this and gives them a means for reconnecting with their families when they are released.

In the F.A.T.H.E.R.S. program at San Quentin (which was briefly described in Chapter 1), one of the prisoners enrolled in the program because he was soon to be released to the custody of his sister. She wanted to help him but was concerned about his influence on her four children. The brother completed the family literacy program and left prison with children's books he had carefully selected, one for each of his nieces and nephews.

Two months later the sister wrote to the program expressing her gratitude for what had been done for her and her brother. Her children had loved the books and their uncle had readily reconnected to them by reading to them. She was proud to say that her brother was a very positive influence in her children's lives because of all he had learned in the F.A.T.H.E.R.S. program. He was looking forward to soon being allowed to visit his own children.

HOMELESS SHELTERS

Of all the special populations, the homeless are probably the most challenging to serve. They tend to be transient and often must move from shelter to shelter because of time limitations imposed by these facilities. They also have more immediate needs than even the incarcerated have, such as where to sleep that night and how to feed and clothe their children.

But homeless families need family literacy programs, too. Providing services to them must, however, take into account their special needs and see that the ideas and suggestions provided to them make sense within their situation.

Some libraries are hesitant to provide library cards for homeless families because they do not have an address and may not return materials. This can be a real impediment to providing needed family literacy services to the homeless. Hopefully you can convince your library to at least provide lending services of children's books for homeless families. If you partner closely with a shelter, you may be able to provide (from donations) a library of children's books that can stay at the shelter. In this way the family can easily access the books while residing there.

While consulting with a number of different homeless programs in the early years of the implementation of the McKinney Act grants, this author experienced firsthand the difficulties faced by homeless families. Telling a single mother of three young children about the importance of reading to her children every day did not seem to make a lot of sense in her harried world. In order to motivate these families, I needed a more practical approach.

I asked these homeless parents when were the most difficult times that they spent with their children. One mother of three youngsters under age five told me those were the times when she had to wait in line for her welfare check, or food stamps, or public transportation. I suggested that she take some of the children's books from the shelter the next time she had to wait in line.

About six weeks later I returned to the shelter and that mother of three was still there. She was so excited to see me and could not wait to tell me of her experiences. She had taken my advice while waiting in line at a health clinic for shots for her youngest. She took out her books and began to read to her children. Soon all the children at the clinic were beginning to gather around her. When she had read the four books she had brought, the children begged to hear them again.

This homeless mother was so proud. She had not only kept her own children quiet and occupied for the long wait but had entertained others as well. Her eyes shone with pride as she told me the story. The nurses at the clinic asked if she would bring books when she came back the next time. She felt respected, needed, and valued—and she was! Not only did her children and the other children visiting the clinic benefit from her efforts, but her own self-esteem was greatly enhanced.

TEEN PARENTS

Like the other special populations, teenage parents often need family literacy services but these young parents can be very difficult to serve. Many of them lack basic literacy skills and often were raised in homes that did not value or model literacy as an important part of everyday life. These teens, like the homeless, have numerous other interests and needs that can conflict with their ability to provide literacy activities for and with their children.

Providing all the components of family literacy for teenagers may be beyond the scope of what a public library can address. However, partnering with another agency that already provides educational services for minor parents can be very successful and enable the library to reach a population of potential library patrons and their young children.

Contra Costa County Library in California has worked successfully with the Minor Parent program at a local adult school for many years. One day each week these teen mothers have their children with them all day. The library's FFL coordinator goes to the class at the adult school on that day each week for eight weeks and provides storytimes, crafts, games, songs, books, and other literacy-enhancing activities. At the end of the eight weeks the entire class, mothers and children, are bused to the local library by the school district. Their two hours of program activities include: being introduced to the library in general and to the children's librarian and children's area specifically; receiving a library card for themselves and each child; listening to a special storytime presented by the children's librarian; and discovering that the library can be a fun, interesting place.

Salinas Public Library, in the agricultural Central Valley of California, has a very successful partnership with the Salinas Adult School to provide family literacy services for the teen mothers in the school. Maria Roddy, literacy coordinator at the library, began the program with an LSCA Title I grant and has continued it with library, school, and state FFL funding.

Melissa, a teen mom in this program, praised the program and what it has done for her. "I enjoy taking my son to parenting classes because they not only teach you how to love a child, but how to raise a child and guide his way in life. Another thing that I liked is the FFL story hour at the library. I never thought my son would enjoy it until I saw in his face that expression of enjoyment, and how he was very entertained. As of today, things in my life have improved! I picture myself as a good parent because I know that I spend time with my child."

Another teen parent, Maribel, summed up her experiences. "The Families for Literacy program gives us time to spend with our children and actually sit down with them. It gets us started as to how to use the library and how to get books. We also get to meet other parents. We learn things from each other. We read to our children, and we become better readers. The books we get to take home are so great and at home we read them over and over again!"

IN SUMMARY

Funding is not always easy to obtain, but family literacy is a program that does appeal to many funders of different types. Targeting special populations may also make it easier to obtain funds. Special populations may be a challenge to serve, but they can also be some of the most rewarding groups with whom to work. Generally the library will find it worth the extra effort to serve these groups.

Remember that additional funding is not always necessary. As I have trained libraries and other agencies throughout the country in the basics of family literacy, I often use an exercise in which I divide the participants into four or more small groups. Each small group is designated a specific amount of money and asked to plan a one-year family literacy program with a budget of $25,000, $10,000, $3,000, or no money at all. Believe it or not, the most creative, collaborative, and innovative program designs from each workshop are those by the groups that were given no money.

7 WILL ANYONE SHOW UP?

> Our retention strategy is primarily to inspire tutors to be creative and energetic in responding to their students' family libraries. We give away paperbacks monthly to each child in the learner's family, a birthday book for every child, and a monthly hardcover book for the family. We provide family storytimes/parties monthly and have food to share there. Some families who do not regularly attend, will come when a birthday book is waiting for their child.
>
> —Robin Levy, San Rafael (California) Public Library's Families for Literacy coordinator

---

RECRUITING AND RETAINING FAMILIES

One thing to remember from the beginning is that there is no single, right way to do recruitment and that what works for some programs/ libraries/communities does not necessarily work for another. California had 59 state-funded, library-based family literacy programs in 1998–99. Although they shared many similarities, they also had many differences. The bottom line is to find out what works best for your library and your community and use it!

TWELVE SUGGESTIONS FOR RECRUITMENT

1. **Target your audience.** Know whom you want to reach. The more specific you can be, the easier will be your recruitment. You might choose to target low-income families, teen parents, new moms, or parents with children of specific ages. You may decide to target Head Start families in a particular community. Be guided by the needs of your community, as discovered through your needs assessment, and the resources of your library and potential family literacy program.
2. **Collaborate with other community agencies that serve your target group.** Although this was discussed more thoroughly in Chapter 5, it needs to be mentioned again here. Clients are a wonderful resource that collaborating agencies can share. Some of your best recruiters will be the staff in other agencies who can sell your program to their clients. Participants in other programs who recognize the value of family literacy and are willing to promote it to their neighbors and fellow participants are also excellent at recruitment.
3. **Get the buy-in of your library staff and administration.** For library-based family literacy programs to succeed, the entire library must work together to recruit and support the families and enrich their use of the library. Your library staff must en-

dorse the program or else the environment within the library will not be conducive to the development of a quality, effective, enduring program. Include the family literacy staff as part of the children's and youth services team. Chapter 3 discusses the importance of commitment from the entire library to the start-up of a program, but this same commitment can be crucial to recruitment also.

4. **Give the families something that appeals to them.** For most of your target families, books and libraries will not be something that "turns them on." Many of these parents never had fun with books or stories and have no reason to believe that their children, let alone themselves, will enjoy such activities. According to San Leandro's FFL coordinator and children's librarian Penny Peck, "Books may be great to most of us, but they can also be like eating healthy food or getting socks for Christmas. Plan for other free 'stuff' as incentives too!"

Don't expect to recruit these families with "storytimes" in the library. You may be planning a storytime, but call it a "party," or a snow day, or a family circus or zoo and use that theme. Always keep in mind that the most compelling reason adults bring their families in to participate is so that their children will not have to go through what they have experienced. They want a better life and more opportunities for their children than they had. These are the types of opportunities your program wants to provide.

One popular theme in sunny Menlo Park, California, has been a snow day. Families are invited to the library where a truckload of shaved ice has been dumped on the lawn. Old socks are washed and used as mittens for the children as they play in the "snow." Books with a snow or snowman theme are read. For many of these children (and even some of the adults) this is the only experience they have ever had with "snow." Snacks include fruit juice snowcones and snowmen sandwiches. Plan family events that you know your target audience will respond to. If you don't know what these are—-ask them!

5. **Computers are exciting and appealing to children and adults alike.** Computers can be wonderful incentives for getting families to participate in your program, if you can make them available. Children are often more comfortable with computers and may learn more quickly than their parents. Educational software that has family and age appropriate themes is available and sometimes even free. Families easily write and publish their own stories together using a computer.

The Internet can also be a wonderful tool for families to explore together. They can look up information on their favorite authors or characters in a book. They can research their family genealogy. The uses of the Internet are almost endless.

6. **Go to where the families are.** Take your first programs into the community to an area where your audience already congregates or lives. Begin initial programs at *their* sites. It takes a great deal of energy and commitment for adults to get children ready and bring them to the library or another site with which they may not be familiar or comfortable. Go to where they already are. Then, when these families are "hooked on your books" and "stimulated by your stories," bring them into the library at times convenient to them.

   Susan Gabbine, the FFL coordinator at Richmond (Calif.) Public Library described their successful recruitment techniques in their 1997/98 FFL Final Report:

   > We do extensive outreach into the community, making presentations at preschool parent meetings, teen mom groups, single parent groups, local community service groups, local churches, etc., wherever we may find prospective new learners with age appropriate children.

   > We stock the Richmond Public Library and the Library Bookmobile with flyers and pass out flyers at a variety of community events, such as local trade shows and city sponsored events. We have provided written materials that have been published in the city newspaper as well as in local area newspapers and advertising publications (unpublished internal report).

7. **Involve your target audience in your planning from the beginning.** Invite some people from your target audience to help you in planning your family literacy program. Listen to what they want and when and where they want it. You do not have to be ruled by every concern that they express, but you should recognize that they are the best people to direct these decisions. Just because they lack some literacy skills, do not assume that they lack thinking skills. They may need help in organizing and expressing their thoughts, but they are adults with many other skills and life experiences. Too many literacy programs develop programs, services, and materials without ever asking the learner/client/patron what he/she wants and needs.

8. **Convince key people in the target audience.** If you can reach and recruit the people with influence (influence brokers) in the target community first, they may be your best recruitment tool. It may take time to win their confidence but it will be well worth any time you spend with these important people. Time spent with them at the beginning can save much time and energy later.

The SPCA's horse and wagon help take the programs to where the families are in Riverside, California.

9. **Do *not* rely on *print* to recruit.** You are trying to reach a population that is not a reading population. Print, flyers, posters, and other traditional tools of promoting library programs may not be very effective. Use a multimedia approach and personal contacts.

A short video that tells the true story of an adult who has stepped forward to learn to read can be very motivating. *Enrique's Story*, available through the California State Library Foundation in Sacramento, is one example. It is short (7.5 minutes) yet moving. Low-literacy adults will see themselves in this story about another learner. It isn't easy to learn to read as an adult. This video makes it clear that it takes time and dedication but that the library is an ideal place to go. It promotes literacy in the adult roles of parent/family member and worker.

When you do use print, use plain, straightforward English with as few words as possible. Use mostly words of one or two syllables. A Fact Sheet on using plain English for family literacy recruitment is available from the Public Information Office, American Library Association, 50 East Huron Avenue, Chicago, IL 60611; pio@ala.org.

If you decide to use the media to reach your audience, choose one that makes sense. Use a Spanish language radio station to reach Spanish-speaking adults. Use an Asian-language newspaper to reach potential Asian learners. Even though most adult learners do not read a newspaper, someone important in their lives probably does and will relay the information.

Although public services announcements (PSAs) are no longer required, many radio and television stations still play them. Provide written PSAs of varying lengths, usually ten seconds, twenty seconds, and thirty seconds. Send them out on a regular basis. Remember that January is often a down time with little paid advertising, freeing up more time for "freebies."

In any messages to the media, always provide the name of an appropriate contact person who will be available. Cultivate media staff. Thank them when they do play your messages. Let them know that you got results.

One caution about general media releases. Be sure you are prepared to handle the results. You may get many calls and visitors, appropriate and not. If you have targeted your client population very specifically, media releases to the general public may not be a good idea.

10. **Emphasize FREE, FUN, FOOD!** Whether using print or other media, emphasize that your program will be free and fun and that **food** will be part of the program. Food is a wonderful incentive. It does not have to be expensive or involved, but food not only acts as an initial recruitment tool, it also helps bring participants back. Some of the FFL programs found out very early that serving food was an excellent way to attract people who had been reluctant to come into the library. Some even serve the food first to ensure that families arrive on time!

11. **Use your volunteers and tutors wisely.** Include tutors or other volunteers in your planning and involve them and their children in your programs. Tutors can be a key element in the success of any family literacy program. Also involve tutors (and teachers) in recruiting their learners and their families. Use them to help bring these families into your program.

Volunteers who are trained to tutor adults prior to the establishment of your family literacy program, however, may not always understand the importance of family literacy to these families. Volunteers value literacy and understand the critical role that it plays in the lives of their adult students. They are often, however, so focused on the immediate needs of the adults whom they are tutoring that they may have to be not only trained in family literacy, but also convinced to make it a part of their tutoring.

Make sure that tutors understand that they will not be using *only* children's books with their adult literacy student but that these books are valuable components of the overall instructional program. Don't be surprised if previously trained volunteers at first consider the family literacy programming and focus to be an interference in their adult literacy work.

12. **Get the names and addresses of the children and send program invitations personally to the child.** There is nothing harder than to say no to a child who has just received a personal invitation in the mail to attend an event or a party. Most adults will find it very difficult not to agree to accompany the invited child to the program. Getting them there the first time is actually the hardest job. Once there, make the event so enjoyable that they just cannot stay away. Keep a record of the birth dates of the children and send special greetings and invitations to the birthday child.

SIX RECRUITMENT LESSONS FROM CALIFORNIA'S FFL PROGRAMS

It is more difficult than expected for most libraries to recruit adult learners with low literacy skills into family literacy programs. The reasons for this are varied, but here are some of those that have been suggested:

- Parents who need family literacy often also contend with many other problems, such as unemployment or underemployment, single-parent households, and so forth. Making the additional commitment in time and energy needed for family literacy activities appears to them to be a luxury rather than a necessity. They will have other priorities.
- These parents don't necessarily see the connection between their low literacy skills and future learning difficulties for their children. They may view the school as *the* only place where learning occurs and must be educated about the importance of the preschool years in developing language and preliteracy skills. They may not understand the critical role that they play in advocating for and supporting their school-age children. Moreover, tutors are often not aware of this importance either, especially with respect to infants and preschoolers.
- Many of these parents fear public exposure of their lack of literacy skills and the accompanying social stigma. They want to seek help for their children but are reluctant to reveal themselves as adults with limited literacy by attending programs.

- Distance, lack of private or public transportation, and time constraints offer substantial barriers to both adult and family literacy programs. It is important to take this into consideration when planning location and time of events.

- Most parents want to help their children with the skills that lead to reading, but many are not prepared to seek help in improving their own literacy. Even when children are the parents' primary source of positive self-esteem and the children's needs are paramount, these same parents' lack of confidence in reading and education can prevent them from seeking literacy help for themselves.

- Adult learners are as concerned as any parent about the language development and readiness for reading in their children, but they often lack both skills and confidence in this area. These parents do not perceive themselves as "teachers" of their young children and do not know how to make education a primary value in their home.

TWELVE SUGGESTIONS FOR RETENTION

1. **Make your programs so fun and exciting that the children will insist on coming back.** The whole family will fall in love with books, even the older siblings, when wonderful children's books and stories are presented by dedicated and enthusiastic readers and storytellers. Not only will the families come back, but if the programs are appealing enough they will also bring their friends, neighbors, and relatives.

   Penny Peck, San Leandro (Calif.) Public Library, believes that their programs are a key to the successful retention of their families. In her 1997/98 FFL Final Report, Penny writes:

   > Having consistent FFL staff conduct the monthly Storytime sessions is a key element to success and retention of consistent learner participation. One children's librarian, special FFL volunteers, and literacy staff always provide personal service and a "comfort level" in the physical set-up of Storytime. Book distribution and Storytime sessions are held in a consistent manner. Personal selection of Bonus Books [free books the children select themselves] facilitates "book excitement." Special events especially increased participation this past year—for example, Christmas Family Photos, January Pizza Party, and the Police Officer visitation.

2. **Provide culturally diverse materials.** Have stories and books mirror the cultures of your audience as well as the experiences of those from other cultures. There is great intrinsic value in these adults and children seeing themselves and their culture reflected in books. Use other languages and cultures to make your pro-

grams a learning experience for all involved—parents, children, and tutors/teachers. Children's books are rich sources of cultural diversity. Use them to their fullest.

A few years ago the San Rafael Public Library planned a storytime with a Filipino theme. Staff made a special point to call their Filipino families and encourage them to attend. Food and children's books from the Philippines were also featured. A guest storyteller was invited who told traditional tales of the islands and taught attendees to count and sing in Tagalog.

Much to the dismay of staff, the families who showed up for the event that day were Asian and Latino. Not one of the Filipino families arrived. Staff was disappointed and feared the event would be a failure. However, that was not the case.

The Asian and Latino adult learners, their families, and their tutors all became enthralled by the program. They loved the Filipino stories and were soon learning to sing and count in Tagalog. Tutors later said that they thought the event was one of their most successful ever because they were modeling adult learning behaviors along with their adult learners. Everyone was on the same level and learning something new at the same time.

3. **Involve your parents in the planning/programming so that they have ownership of the program.** Give parents "group support time" separate from the children so that they can discuss parenting issues of concern to them, but keep it short and make sure that all the parents are involved. You do not have to teach lessons on parenting skills! Let the parents discuss these issues as they evolve from stories read. Emphasize the importance of family interaction—the parent as the child's first teacher. Validate the parents' own experiences. See Chapter 8 for more information on using children's books as catalysts for parenting discussions.

In Butte County, California, the library's family literacy actively involves parents in each storytime/party. Parents are asked to serve refreshments, help the smaller children with gluing and cutting, arrange chairs, take small groups of children outdoors to do "messy" craft or science projects, or any number of other tasks. Their family literacy coordinator reported, "Because parents felt needed, they made an effort to attend."

4. **Use incentives.** Incentives are aids both to retention and to recruitment. Give the families something they can take with them and use at home. Make every effort to provide a variety of incentives that appeal to your population.

Free books are one of the most effective incentives. Quality new or used children's books are very popular. Hardback books

Documentaries such as *Enrique's Story* can help recruit learners and tutors for your program. Enrique and his family are similar to many who participate in family literacy programs.

are great but expensive. Many of the classic and more popular books also now come in paperback. By purchasing a mix of hardback and paperback books, the program can help the family to build its own library. Building a home library instills a sense of pride of ownership in the children and helps them to value and appreciate books more.

Provide craft materials such as crayons, paper, scissors, glue, tape, and pencils for your families. A variety of materials can be packaged in zip-together plastic bags and sent home as an activity of the program. Do not assume that such materials are already in the homes of your families. Do not assume that these parents know the importance of providing such material or of engaging their children in craft-type activities.

Supply ideas for using materials that are already found at home. Such things as milk and egg cartons, plastic jugs and bottles, and glass jars are usually in the home. Parents just need help in seeing how and why these can be used to enhance literacy skills.

Take photos of your families working and reading together at your programs and give them to the families to take home. Help them create photo albums of all their activities through the course of your programming. These photos serve as a reminder to the family of the fun they had at that program and will make them more eager to return.

Provide certificates of achievement or attendance. Use discount coupons and free prizes donated from local restaurants and merchants as incentives.

Remember to make food or meals a part of your programs whenever possible!

5. **Make sure that your library is a warm, welcoming place.** Do whatever is necessary to ensure that a family's first experience is a positive one. Train all staff in how to identify low-literacy adults and how to respond to their questions with tact and ease. Alert them to such possible indicators as an adult who asks for help because "I forgot my reading glasses." All patrons should be treated with kindness and respect, but special care should be taken with these new and unsure library users.

    Many of these parents may never have been in a library before and will be uncertain what to expect. Some will have unrealistic expectations of how their children should act in the library or during a program or event. One family literacy coordinator always takes her own young children to programs so that the literacy families can see that the coordinator's children do not behave perfectly either!

    Sell your own library staff on the program and keep them informed. Make sure that they don't view this program as just an additional burden. Sensitize your staff to the needs of your target audience and make them aware of this neglected and at risk group. Integrate family literacy into your regular library services.

6. **Teach your parents how to use the library.** Teach the adults how to select books for their children. Try using color-coded stickers on the bindings of children's books to make it easier for parents to know the reading difficulty of the books. If you help these adults and children use the library with ease and pleasure—they will be library users for life, not just for the life of your family literacy program.

7. **Do follow up.** If a family who has attended misses a program, call and find out why. What do they need to make it possible for them to attend the next program? Let them know that you care and that you missed them.

8. **Make each program as inclusive as possible so if a family does not return, they still have a valuable experience to carry away from even just one meeting.** Given the myriad problems and issues with which these families must contend, do not be surprised if some of the families are not able to attend your family literacy programs, no matter how exciting and fun you make them. Be sure that every event or program that you plan has specific goals and that you achieve them. Then, even if a family attends only once, you can be confident that they will have gained something valuable and enduring.

9. **Always remember that events must be FOCUSED, FLEXIBLE, and FAST moving.** Always focus on what you are doing and why. At the same time, be flexible so that if something is clearly not working with a particular group, you have an alternate plan and move into it quickly.

    Keep up the pace. Children have short attention spans and so do many adults. Put these children and adults together and the collective attention span can be even shorter.

10. **Involve new learners in family literacy activities even if they must wait for a tutor.** Involving the entire family in a family literacy program can be a great retention technique for keeping adults involved with their own literacy improvement. An adult learner from San Leandro Community Library tried working with three different tutors, but for various reasons none of them seemed to work out. During this time, however, the learner was very faithful about bringing her 14-month-old daughter to family literacy storytimes. Numerous other obstacles and problems ensued, including changes at work and the birth of a new baby. When the mother was unable to attend, the father brought the older child to the library. Staff continued to work with the family and encourage the mother to return to tutoring. Even though her life remained hectic, the mother eventually decided she was ready to go back to tutoring and to get a nurse's certificate. If she had not been kept involved and encouraged through the family literacy activities, she would probably have dropped out of the literacy program altogether.

11. **Fathers: Do all you can to invite them and encourage their participation.** Too often family literacy programs and activities are attended only by mothers, even when it is the father who is the adult literacy student. Do all you can to support and invite the child's father (or father figure). Help make him comfortable by having male staff involved in the programming whenever possible. Ask a father active in the program to make calls to other families encouraging their attendance and asking specifically

to speak with the father. Feature books which focus on the father/child relationship.

At Corona (Calif.) Public Library, John Zickefoose, the FFL coordinator, is a father and former adult learner in the program. John's visibility in the program automatically makes other males feel more comfortable and welcome. John personally calls each father often during the course of a series of programs to invite him and make him feel important to the program.

Have a really special event just for fathers and their children. Use incentives that will be difficult for fathers to resist, such as sports tickets or the attendance of a special local sports star. Make a special effort to show fathers that they are wanted and needed in the family literacy program.

12. **Home visits can aid program effectiveness.** Santa Clara County (Calif.) has found that home visits by Susan Lewis, the family literacy coordinator, can be very helpful. During the six-week break between program sessions, Susan visits each family, usually in their home. She is careful to schedule home visits at a time when the children will also be home. Visits include a book giveaway for the children; book sharing time with the family; and, a chat with the adult learner about how tutoring has been going, whether the program is meeting the learner's needs and the children's needs, whether something can be done to improve the program, what guest speakers they would like to hear, what future themes they would like, and a review of the upcoming session schedule.

In her 1997/98 FFL final report, Susan stated,

We have found that learners are more likely to express their true feelings about our program in this one-on-one informal setting. Because of this improved communication, we believe that we have been able to shape the program to fit our families' needs resulting in a high retention rate. Home visits are labor intensive (two hours to prepare and carryout each visit), but . . . are worth it.

TRAINING TUTORS FOR FAMILY LITERACY

Volunteer tutors can be a very crucial component of any family literacy program. Whether they are your library volunteers who wish to tutor or volunteers from one of your collaborating partners, they need specific guidance in providing family literacy tutoring. Even when the adult literacy component is being provided by credentialed teachers in a partnering agency, those teachers will more than likely need special training in the basic components of family literacy because they were probably hired as adult education teachers and may know little about family literacy.

The remainder of this chapter will set forth some basic guidelines and suggestions for providing family literacy tutor training. Although a variety of approaches for training literacy tutors for adults have been developed, it has yet to be conclusively proven that any one method, technique, or material is always best. This section will not attempt to resolve that issue.

As a reading specialist and tutor trainer of over 2,000 volunteer tutors, I recommend that every program take a learner-centered, eclectic approach to tutor training which teaches tutors to recognize and enhance the learning strengths and styles of their learners in a flexible and pleasant manner.

Reading should be enjoyable, and learning to read or improving one's reading should be enjoyable also! If the process is not fun, then it is less likely that the adult and his or her children will come to enjoy books and read for the pure pleasure of reading. Chapter 8 deals in detail with how to make literacy improvement fun by using children's books for both the adult and the child. Always keep in mind that the best way to improve one's reading is to read!

Integrate and specifically point out family literacy teachings throughout tutor training but require tutors assigned to families to also take an additional, more thorough training specifically in the basic components of family literacy.

Some basic family literacy concepts that need to be taught to tutors and teachers include the following:

- **Family literacy is a program that serves the whole family.** It provides for the literacy needs of the adult, the emerging literacy needs of the children, intergenerational activities around literacy, and opportunities for discussion and reading about sound parenting.
- **Illiteracy is a cycle.** It passes from generation to generation. "Children whose parents are functionally illiterate are twice as likely as their peers to be functionally illiterate." (NAEP, 1985)[1]
- **The adult should be the primary focus of the family literacy program.** If the literacy attitudes, skills, and habits of the adult are not changed, then the literacy model in the home will not support the literacy needs of the growing child.
- **Reading aloud works.** Children must be read to at the earliest possible age, even prenatally, and this should continue as an activity until the child is 12 or 13 and beyond. "The single most important activity for building the knowledge required for eventual success in reading is reading aloud to children." (Anderson,

1985, 23).[2] Children should read aloud to their parents and others as soon as they are able.

- **Parents need to model reading.** They need to understand that valuing reading and modeling reading and writing in the home is the best way to ensure that their children will become readers. "A parent is a child's first tutor in unraveling the fascinating puzzle of written language. A parent is a child's one enduring source of faith that somehow, sooner or later, he or she will become a good reader." (Anderson, 28)[3]

- **Adults also need to do more overt teaching of their children.** As important as modeling is, it is not the only factor. Adults need to spend more time talking with their children and giving them opportunities for a variety of experiences. Appendix D gives a short, easy-to-read set of guidelines to help parents with limited reading skills understand how to lead their children to reading.

- **Family literacy learning is not one way.** At the same time the child is learning from the adult, the adult is also learning from the child. Tutors and teachers often comment on how much they learn from their students. Parents as teachers, especially those parents with limited literacy skills, find that they too learn as they teach.

- **Parental involvement in their children's education is critical.** Parents with limited literacy, however, are often afraid of a system that they may perceive as having failed them. This fear can keep them from expressing the interest and concern that they feel about their child's own education. They may also erroneously view the school as the only place where learning takes place.

- **Parents are the ultimate authorities on their own children.** Tutors should emphasize the strengths of the parents and help them develop their own well thought out standards for what they want to model for their children. If a program is to be learner centered, tutors must listen to the parents' needs with regard to their children and model lesson plans around these needs. Family literacy issues will arise naturally with this style of tutoring.

- **The tutor uses activities with the adult learner to reach the children.** The tutor's goal is to empower parents to be their child's first teacher. Whether they *want* to be or *are prepared* to be, parents are indeed role models and teachers for their children. Tutor training should emphasize this so that the tutor will be able to help the parents understand this critical role.

- **Tutors model teaching for the adults.** As tutors work with the adults, they should constantly say, "You can use this method/book/activity at home with your children." The tutor needs to demystify "teaching" so that the learners/parents can emulate the tutor when working with their children.

- **Tutors should teach to the *strengths* of the adult learner and of the family.** Help the adult to see that just coming forward as an adult to learn to read or improve literacy skills demonstrates a great deal of courage. These adults have accomplished much in their lives but often see only their failures. The tutor should help them focus on their accomplishments and value their successes. If the adults are taught this way, they will learn to relate to their children in a similar manner.
- **Language Experience Approach (LEA) stories are one very effective way that tutors can involve both parents and children in literacy activities.** The learners might relate stories to the tutor to write down; the learners can then take the written stories home and read them to their children. Blank books or journals can be sent home for the parents and children to write in together. Family history is important and should be recorded. Anecdotes about the family and stories around family photos or children's art can all be incorporated into the LEA.
- **Literacy is more than just reading. Literacy is reading *and* writing.** Tutors/teachers need to help parents become more comfortable with the writing process so that they will be able to make their children feel good about their own writing. It is not often that adult learners say, "I cannot read." One most likely hears "I can't read well" or "I can read but I don't understand what I am reading." But it is not unusual at all to hear adult learners say, "I can't write." The fact is, they *can* write, but they are generally even more intimidated by writing than they are by reading. This same attitude toward writing is often perpetuated in their children.
- **Trainers should use children's books with the tutors during training.** Use the books as examples for specific skill practices. Use them for practice in lesson planning. Give each tutor or small group of tutors a different children's book and ask them to create a lesson plan around that book. Create hypothetical learner profiles and situations that include adults with children of specific ages. Have the tutors present their work to the whole group.
- **Trainers should discuss with the tutors when and how literacy begins.** Explain that it is an aspect of the development of language and thus begins when language begins, with the first senses, like hearing. Ask them about their first experiences with books and reading. Were they read to as children? If they were read to, what are the feelings that arise when they think back to those moments? Most literacy volunteers have very warm, clear memories of being read to. It is part of the reason why many of them came to be avid readers themselves. Help them to understand that reading aloud can provide positive, family interaction and

a nurturing and closeness for the family members who participate. This is one way that books come to be associated with wonderful memories and thus become loved.

- **Tutors should receive some basic training in how to choose children's books.** The tutors will then be able to help their learners make informed choices. Ask your children's librarian to help with this portion of the training. It is also very helpful for the tutors as well as the learners to become familiar with the children's librarian so that they will be comfortable going to him/her to seek help when they need it.

- **Your program and your tutors should accept and value the culture and language of the family.** Encourage adults to use their other language as well as English with their children. Never lose sight of the richness of another culture. Even when it is second- or third-generation American, the family reflects the culture of its heritage, neighborhood, and life.

  Bilingual children's books are a culturally rich resource for family literacy programs. Only a few years ago, good bilingual books were very limited. Cultural sensitivity and the changing demographics of our country have changed that. Now it is possible to find both classic and new bilingual quality children's literature in a myriad of languages.

- **Family literacy programs should accept the presence of television and help families to make the best possible use of its programming.** Television is a part of the lives of 98 percent of the families in the United States, and it is doubtful that this will change anytime in the near future.

  Milton Chen, author of *The Smart Parent's Guide to Kids' TV* (1994), states that "Television cannot be blamed for the problems of poverty, but it can be part of the solution to improving the lives of children at risk. . . . But TV will not work to serve children without the involvement of parents . . . "[4] Bill Moyers also touts the educational value of television. "Once I thought the most important political statement we could make about television was to turn it off. But television can instruct, inform, and inspire, as well as distract, distort, and demean. And turning it off rejects the good with the bad."[5]

  Because television is an important part of communication development and learning for most children, parents need to be taught and encouraged to use it positively with their children. According to Chen, "The amount of time American children spend watching TV is staggering: an average of 4 hours a day, 28 hours a week, 1,400 hours a year, close to 18,000 hours by the time a child graduates from high school."[6] Parents need to control the use of television and get involved in what their children watch. Tutors and teachers should give parents an opportunity to discuss the shows their children watch openly and honestly, and help them develop their own guidelines for what shows their children can and cannot watch.

Family literacy programs can take children's natural fascination with television and use that to promote books and reading. Such shows as *Sesame Street*, the *Puzzle Place*, *Mr. Rogers' Neighborhood*, *Tots TV*, and *Storytime* all build basic skills and fill important needs for children. *Storytime*, a production of KCET in which mostly famous people read a book to a group of children and interact with them, was developed with input from educators and librarians. It further reinforces the importance of books and libraries with a tag line at the end of each episode telling the children that their local library has more books like the one read on the show.

- Trainers should model the techniques and philosophies they want their tutors to use with learners. If you want learner-centered, goal-oriented, interactive tutoring, then you must apply these same standards to your training of the tutors. Don't just tell them what to do; model it yourself throughout the training they receive. See Appendix E for some examples of tutor training agendas.

Berlin and Sum (1988), in their report *Toward a More Perfect Union: Basic Skills, Poor Families and Our Economic Future*, state, "Because of this intergenerational effect of the parents' education on the child's, it is unlikely that we will be able to make a major difference for the child unless we place equal priority on education and academic remediation for the parent."[7]

Although I basically agree with this statement, the past 15 years of literacy work has led me more and more to the belief that the literacy skill levels of the parent are not as important as the literacy attitudes and habits practiced by the adult in the home. It is, of course, best that adults have adequate literacy skills, but even parents with limited skills can be taught to promote literacy in the home and to interact with the child's school in a confident way.

A positive and supportive attitude and the ensuing literacy-rich home environment can have a profound effect on the emerging literacy of children. It is possible that the educational level of the parent in the Berlin and Sum study had as much to do with the attitudes and habits in the home as with the actual literacy skill level of the adults.

- A National Governor's Association study determined that when parents are involved in their preschoolers' educational programs, those children eventually showed:

31% reduction in juvenile corrections rates
35% greater high school graduation rates
36% higher employment levels
45% lower adolescent pregnancy rates
90% fewer special education placements[8]

The library-based family literacy programs in California have found that the most effective way to train tutors in the concepts of family literacy is to integrate the training throughout the regular adult literacy tutor training. Although not all tutors will work with learners who have children at home, all adult learners have children in their lives, either their own or those of relatives, neighbors, or friends, and thus can be reading models for these children. In addition, it is helpful to all tutors to understand how and when literacy develops so that they can help their learners understand better their problems with literacy. Adult learners appreciate this insight into their own literacy difficulties.

After a thorough introduction to the basic concept in their initial tutor training, tutors matched with families can be brought back for a more in-depth training in family literacy. For a sample of a typical, in-depth Family Literacy Tutor Training Agenda from one of California's FFL programs, see Appendix E.

EQUIPPED FOR THE FUTURE

Equipped for the Future (EFF) is a National Institute for Literacy (NIFL) program that is seeking to define what it is that adults need to know in their major life roles of parent/family member, worker, and citizen/community member. NIFL began by asking adult learners around the country to explain their needs and goals and these three roles emerged. It was clear that the demands of these roles were changing and that adult learners wanted to be better prepared to fulfill these roles now and in the future.

EFF is especially significant for family literacy tutor training because it clearly identifies the parent/family member role as a major focus for most adult learners. EFF starts from the premise that adults are themselves best able to define their literacy needs and goals and that they should be instrumental in designing their own learning. This philosophy fits very well with the learner-centered, goal-based adult literacy provided by most public libraries. EFF further validates the importance of and necessity for family literacy programs.

The philosophic basis of EFF should be a component of tutor training in family literacy. It can help tutors and learners set goals, identify benchmarks along the way, and evaluate their eventual success. Four public libraries in California were field development sites for EFF in 1998 and again in 1999.

As example of an EFF activity, participants in a literacy-parenting class in the Santa Clara County Library program selected the skill "listen actively," which they used during class. They defined benchmarks for how they knew they were using that skill well. Responses included, "I don't have to think about what I'm going to say next" and "I'm not talking all the time." The learners were practicing the role of parent/family member. Learners then discussed ways they could practice and use this skill across the other two adult roles. For example, as workers, they have to listen actively to their coworkers. One benchmark for success with this skill in the worker role might be the timely completion of a project at work where everybody understood each other and the task at hand.

An article I wrote about Equipped for the Future for the December 1998 issue of *American Libraries* concluded:

> Learners who enter library literacy programs often do so out of an immediate need. They want to read to a young child; they want a better job; they want to be independent. They are already thinking about their lives in terms of the roles identified by EFF. EFF's extensive definition of literacy helps learners recognize the skills they are already using and how those skills apply to different contexts. Literacy instruction begins with what a learner knows, not with what skills he or she lacks. Libraries are ideally suited to use EFF because they already focus on individualized and personalized instruction in which the learner is an equal partner. This partnership is the cornerstone for equipping adult learners for the future.[9]

More information about EFF can be obtained from the National Institute for Literacy in Washington, D.C. and from their Web site at www.nifl.gov.

WHEN A FAMILY CAN'T ATTEND SPECIAL PROGRAMMING AT THE LIBRARY

Not all families who need family literacy will be able to attend the special programs that the library provides. Work and class schedules, transportation problems, children's extracurricular activities, homework, bedtime, illness, and fear of the unfamiliar (the library) are all valid reasons why families cannot or will not attend.

Another important issue for some learners is that by asking learners to attend a library program with others present, the library asks them to suspend their anonymity. When attending a family program adult learners expose themselves to other adult learners, their families, tutors, and library staff. The learners may fear they will have to explain their low literacy to these other adults or to their own children. This is often most clearly felt in small, close-knit communities where everyone knows everyone else. Anonymity is just not possible. It is important that the family literacy program recognize and respect these issues and limitations.

The following suggestions were expanded and adapted from those made by Beth Bochser, Contra County Library's FFL coordinator, in her final (unpublished) report to the California State Library FY 1992/93. The suggestions concern the involvement of families when they cannot or will not come to events and activities of the family literacy program.

Nine Ways to Include Families

1. Encourage learners to participate in a birthday book program so that at least during those months of the children's birthdays they are making trips to the library. This also ensures that they will meet the children's librarian.
2. Make parenting materials available on an extended loan basis to the tutors.
3. Send Family Storytime materials to the tutor to be reviewed with, and given to, the learners when they cannot or do not attend.
4. Arrange individual library tours for the families with their tutors.
5. Continue to invite the families to all family literacy events, including the special holiday parties.
6. Conduct one-on-one tutoring sessions in the library so that the adult becomes more comfortable in that setting.
7. Have another adult learner in the family literacy program call the families who do not attend to discuss their concerns and see if there are any misconceptions or misunderstandings.
8. Take time to interview the learner and his/her tutor personally in the local library branch. Spending individual time with them initially may alleviate the need for more time-intensive intervention later.
9. Be realistic about the fact that some families simply will not attend programs, but do not exclude them from the other family literacy services because of that.

TUTOR MANUALS

Many programs find it helpful to develop special manuals for their family literacy tutors. These can be distributed and explained at the in-depth family literacy training session and then used by the tutors throughout their tutoring.

The best manuals are designed specifically to meet the needs of a particular community or library. Most contain basic background information about family literacy; pre- and post evaluations or surveys to use with the family; guidelines about developmental stages of children; information about the library itself (hours, staff, location); monthly or quarterly reporting forms for the tutors to send in; information about any special programs (such as the birthday books); parenting materials; bibliographies of children's books for specific ages and needs; and materials for the tutor to use with the adult learner (such as How to Read to Your Child and others).

Tutor manuals are designed to be taken home by tutors and kept as a ready reference guide throughout the course of their tutoring. Some pages can be duplicated and given to the learner after discussion in the tutoring session. These tutor manuals are very popular with volunteer tutors because they provide quick and easy access to important information. A sample of these materials developed by Beth Bochser, Contra Costa County Library, for inclusion in its Families for Literacy Tutor Handbook is found in Appendix F.

NOTES

1. *National Assessment of Educational Progress (NAEP)*. 1985. Washington, D.C.: U.S. Department of Education.
2. Richard C. Anderson, E. H. Hiebert, J. A. Scott, and I. A. G. Wilkinson. 1985. *Becoming a Nation of Readers: The Report of the Commission on Reading*. Washington, D.C.: U.S. Department of Education Commission on Reading.
3. Ibid.
4. Chen, Milton. 1994. *The Smart Parent's Guide to Kids' TV*. San Francisco: KQED BOOKS, xi.
5. Ibid., 82.
6. Ibid., 23.
7. Gordon Berlin and Andrew Sum. 1988. *Toward a More Perfect Union: Basic Skills, Poor Families and Our Economic Future*. New York: Ford Foundation.

8. *Report on Education of the Disadvantaged.* 1981. New York: Webster's International, Inc.

9. Carole Talan. 1998. "Real-Life Empowerment Through Family-Centered Literacy." *American Libraries* 29, no. 11 (December) 49–51.

8 CHILDREN'S BOOKS FOR THE WHOLE FAMILY

> After spending some of each tutoring session reviewing children's books, Lenore had learned how to "put life into reading" to her children. Her whole family now has more fun with books, including her husband, Lenore now looks for books to deal with everyday problems. For example, when her son Brian was teased for wearing glasses, Lenore checked out *Arthur's Eyes*, which had been recommended by the children's librarian. Her son felt much better and not so alone.
> —Beth Bochser writing about Lenore, family literacy parent at Contra Costa County Library's FFL program

USING QUALITY CHILDREN'S BOOKS FOR FAMILY LITERACY

Children's books have always been a wonderful resource. They have never been just for children. Many of the earlier classics in children's literature were actually written as political statements or satires. Every year new, beautiful, emotional, healing, exciting, and fun children's books are published. Why not use them with adult learners?

The sections of this chapter on the rationale for using children's books, selecting books, and reading aloud have been adapted from materials originally created by Elizabeth Segal for the Pittsburgh (Penn.) Free Library's Beginning with Books program.

RATIONALE

Because low-literacy adults have themselves suffered embarrassment or failure on account of inadequate reading and writing skills, they are generally very passionate about not wanting the children in their lives to be exposed to these same traumas and negative experiences. Many adults entering literacy programs state that one of their goals is to read to their children. They do not always realize, however, that reading to their children is also the best way to help these children grow up to be better readers themselves.

In addition, children's books provide something that adult literacy materials do not. They provide practice in the necessary reading skills while at the same time being fun, colorful, and entertaining.

As recently as the 1980s, teachers and tutors were often cautious about using children's materials with an adult learner because these materials might be viewed as insulting or demeaning; however, the attitude with which material of any kind is presented is most likely the attitude the learner will adopt toward that material. In other words, if the tutor/teacher likes the material and presents it as a fun, worthwhile learning resource, then the adult will most likely approach the material with that same attitude. There will always be exceptions, however, and if one should encounter resistance to children's materials, do not use them.

In addition, if an adult has a goal of reading to a child or can be convinced of the value in reading to a child (his/her own child, grandchild, niece or nephew, neighbor, Head Start or daycare child), then using good children's literature in the adult's learning session makes even more sense.

Practicing reading aloud to a child not only increases the adult's reading skills and understanding of literacy development but can boost the adult's self-esteem too. By providing a youngster with the experience of being read to, the adult moves from being part of the literacy problem to being part of the solution.

Quality children's books are visually appealing and use colorful but simple language. They are not contrived (that is, developed to give adults reading practice as are most adult literacy materials), but are written to tell a meaningful story or to convey information in a simple and interesting way. Even though they are written for children, these books often contain nuances discernible only to an adult. They also impart basic morals and life lessons without being "preachy" or "teachy."

When an adult reads consistently to a child, that child generally begins to love books. As the child grows to love storytimes, demands of "read to me" also help ensure that the adult will continue to practice reading between tutoring sessions or classes. Plus, these books are fun and entertaining for both adult and child.

Most children's picture books contain elements of predictability that are of great help to someone just learning to read, whether an adult or a child. Repetitions of phrases, word patterns, and rhymes all help the reader with the text. Colorful and lively illustrations may provide clues to difficult words that the adult encounters and help to teach the use of pictures as clues in all reading.

Also helpful to the adult learner are the concept books that teach basic concepts familiar to adults but often new to the child, such as counting, colors, days of the week, animal names, and so forth. These can be valuable in another way to the limited English or ESL adult who needs to build the concepts of language while at the same time practicing reading skills.

Any adult, even those who do not yet speak or read English, can effectively use wordless picture books. Using the illustrations as clues to the story, adults with no reading skills at all can still share this type of book with a child by telling the story in their own words. These same books can be, however, initially intimidating to adults who think there must be a "right" way to share the book and are unsure what that is. The tutor can help the learner overcome this fear by sharing various interpretations of the same book and explaining that none of them are right or wrong. Only the author knows for sure what was intended, not the reader!

BUILDING A HOME LIBRARY

Experts in the fields of education and literacy have long recognized the value of establishing a home library for families. A public library is a wonderful lifelong resource for books, but a home library is critical to building that special relationship with books that promotes a love of books through ownership.

Author and parent Jim Trelease (1989) introduces his chapter on the relationship of the home and public library to emerging literacy by emphasizing that "Long before children are introduced to their neighborhood public library, books should be a part of their lives. Begin a home library as soon as the child is born."[1]

It has already been recommended in this manual that gift books be part of any family literacy program. These books are a very important aspect of the family experience with literacy. For most families in these programs, the gift books are crucial to their ability to build a home library.

Children's books to give to families can be acquired from a number of different sources. As mentioned earlier, many civic clubs and groups like to donate children's books. Both Nathan's Bagels and Starbucks have book drives each year and donate the books they collect to worthy groups. First Book is a national nonprofit organization that gives disadvantaged children the opportunity to read and own their first new book(s). They work with literacy programs to distribute books to kids.

Reading Is Fundamental (RIF) is also a national nonprofit organization whose mission is to motivate children to read and provide them with books of their own. They reach over three million children each year and are also promoting family literacy. You can learn more about RIF from their web site at www.rif.org.

The National Children's Book and Literacy Alliance (NCBLA) is a newly formed organization founded by children's authors and illustrators. They plan to support literacy initiatives nationwide. More information about this group and its work can be found at www.ncbla.org.

Gift books are an important aspect of the success of California's Families for Literacy (FFL) program. They not only build the pride of ownership in both the children and adults, but they also serve as valuable recruitment and retention tools.

To encourage more reading and get additional books into the homes, Santa Clara County Library conducts a Reading Challenge during each of its FFL six-week sessions. Children are asked to read or have read to them a minimum of five books per week (more if the children are older.) Bulletin boards exhibited at each program show the number of books a family has read and the family's progress toward its reading goal. Each child receives a gift book for meeting the weekly challenge. Participants read approximately 2,805 children's books between July, 1997, and June, 1998. Coordinator Susan Lewis noted, "Parents and children who had been hesitant at the beginning of the program about reading together at home are now proudly waving their Reading Challenge weekly reports as they enter the door on family literacy night. And, even more important, the habit continues between sessions too."

The FFL program library staff became aware early on of one major obstacle that these wonderful gift books presented to the families. Homes where books were not previously found had no space or shelving on which to place these newly acquired and treasured books.

A number of FFL programs now include as one of their first family activities the building of bookshelves for the new families. The building materials are often donated by local merchants or service groups. Some programs have the wood precut by the supplier and ready to be assembled by the families. Families then gather at a suitable location and together assemble and paint the bookshelves. The children provide decorations and help with the painting. Often the names of the children are painted on the shelves. For many programs it is one of their most enjoyable activities and engages the entire family.

In one county library where it was difficult for many of the families to gather at a single site, a local Boy Scout earned his Eagle badge by soliciting the bookshelf materials and preparing them. He then assembled and painted the bookshelves and delivered them personally to each family.

SEVEN CHARACTERISTICS OF HIGH QUALITY CHILDREN'S BOOKS FOR THE ADULT NEW READER

1. The first element to consider in selecting a quality children's book is whether the story is *engaging*.

    The book should be one the adult enjoys. If not, it is doubtful that the child being read to will find the experience pleasurable. Adults with limited literacy skills need to be especially sensitive to this aspect as the process of reading the book aloud must be made to appear fun and relaxed, not tense and strained. Humor appeals to everyone, and adults will generally find books humorous if the teacher/tutor who first introduces them finds them humorous and presents them in that way.

2. The *reading difficulty* of the book should also be considered. Can the adult handle the book with no help or after practice and help from the tutor? The books listed in the Bibliography of Children's Books in Appendix G provide a rough guide to the adult reading level of many of the books in the list. The children's librarian is also a good resource for determining the difficulty of a particular book.

3. Next one should consider the *appropriateness* for the child. Will the book be of interest to a two year old or a five year old? Tutors and parents can be trained to identify interests by age and sex, or they can rely on lists created by their local children's librarian. One should also take into account that children who have not previously been exposed to books in the home often enjoy materials that are developmentally below their actual chronological age.

4. *Illustrations* are important in selecting children's books. Infants and toddlers whose eyes are not yet able to focus on fine lines and pale colors need illustrations that are very large and bright. Bold, primary colors are particularly effective. As children grow older they often appreciate creative, fanciful illustrations. Realistic photos, especially those that portray other children and animals, are always intriguing. Some of the most popular books for babies and toddlers are ones that use actual photographs of babies and toddlers. But a word of caution. Always be sure that the illustrations match the text as both the low literacy adult and the child will find it confusing if they do not.

5. The text should be *fun and not contrived*. Children love humor and nonsense rhymes. They love to play with words and have fun with what they read. One of the reasons children love the works of Dr. Seuss is because of the rhythm, word play, and nonsense words he uses. Younger children particularly like rhyming and repetition. These qualities also help to make the book easier for the adult to read. Be sure that the tutors/teachers and parents understand this.

6. Children also enjoy reading books *about other children like themselves*. Although initially the preferences between the genders is slight, if existent at all, the differences between interests of boys and girls become more pronounced as they get older.

7. Look for *cultural diversity* in a book or books. Select books that expose the child and the adult to the bigger world of

multiethnic, multicultural people and experiences. In recent years a plethora of new books has been published that brings the whole world into the realm of children's books. Many of these are also bilingual, allowing adults to practice reading in both their native language and in English.

Tutors should ask children and adults what they would like to hear or to read. Take a selection of books and try each one out. Then ask them which books were the best. The tutor then uses what he/she learns from this to select more books.

Former FFL Coordinator Nailah Malik (Los Angeles Public Library) provides exciting events for FFL families in Southern California.

READING ALOUD

Most literacy adults will need very specific training and modeling in reading aloud. Some of your tutors and teachers will need this too.

Teach tutors to train their adult learners to use excitement and fun when they read. They should play with the books and with the words. They should learn to interact with the books and the child. If the learner is unsure of a word, a logical substitution is fine. At these initial experiences with books, children and adult learners need to realize that reading does not have to be perfect all the time.

Model what reading aloud can be like in a family of two or four or six. Techniques used by some children's librarians for large-group storytimes are not necessarily the same ones needed when one or more parents sit with one or more children on the lap or couch. Children should be asked questions and be allowed to give responses as they go through the book, especially if the book has been read before. Name things on the page and ask the child to point to them or name the color or tell how many.

Oakland Public Library Director Billie Dancey models the use of quality children's books for Oakland's FFL families.

Remember that children who have not been read to may not initially want to sit still and look at a book. Be patient. In time the child will become interested in looking at what the adult is reading because the adult is interested. It may take time, but don't give up. The adult should continue to read aloud everyday and eventually even the most reluctant child will show interest.

Parents should be cautioned not to become annoyed if a child wants to hear the same book over and over again. Adults may become bored, but clearly the children are getting what they need and want by hearing the book read repeatedly.

Adults also should be read to. Tutors should practice reading aloud to learners. This is not only to model techniques that the learners can use with children but also so that the learner can hear the way books should sound when read with feeling and rhythm. Adults who have not been read to may initially be uneasy with the process, but soon they will enjoy it if the tutor is a good, active reader! Learners should read aloud to their tutors/teachers too.

LIT PAKS

Cindy Costales, an experienced children's librarian and the coordinator of the County of Los Angeles Public Library's literacy program, wanted to create a mechanism that would help parents find it easier to model reading aloud with their children while at the same time extending the reading of books into other family or intergenerational activities. She and her staff developed a series of packets that could be checked out by the parents in her literacy program, taken home for a set time, and used by the family.

These Lit Paks, as they are called, are large folders with pockets that have been decorated and then laminated to help protect them. The decorations can be from the illustrations of the book inside or can be fanciful drawings by staff or children that relate to the theme of the book.

Each Lit Pak contains: a children's book; a simply written guide to reading the book (to be used by the tutor and parent or just by the parent alone); suggestions for extending the theme of the book through specific activities and discussions with the children; and any materials needed to complete a craft or activity.

These packets can be checked out by the parent or the tutor for one month. When they are returned, the literacy staff or volunteers replace any of the consumable items that were contained in the packet and prepare it to be loaned to another family. The packets are inexpensive to develop and to maintain. They could also include a cassette tape of instructions and of a volunteer reading the book aloud if the packet is to be used by a parent with very limited reading ability.

These Lit Paks have been very successful and popular with the families and with the tutors. Other libraries have developed their own or copied them from the County of Los Angeles and now use them in their family literacy programs.

Patricia Smart, former coordinator of literacy at Burbank Public Library, says that the Lit Paks are one of the most successful ideas she has used. She tells of one parent who participated in a parent discussion on "time" after a group reading of the book *Good Night Moon.*

The parent expressed his concern that it was hard for him to find the time to read to his child because he would work all day, come home tired, eat dinner, and want to just relax with the TV or fall asleep in his easy chair. He knew it was important but did not feel he had the time or energy to do it. But, he agreed to take home the Lit Pak that contained the book and read it to his young son.

One month later this man returned the Lit Pak to Patricia with excitement and enthusiasm. He related how his 14-month-old son who had a very limited vocabulary had looked up at the moon one night, pointed at it and said the word "moon" over and over again. This father was very thrilled because he knew that his son had learned this word as he had listened to the book and now was using the word in his own experience. The father now was convinced to make time to read to his son and use other Lit Paks because he had observed first hand that they work!

WHY USE CHILDREN'S BOOKS?

The reasons for using children's books in a family literacy program are almost endless. The following is a summary of just some of the reasons. They are *not* necessarily in order of importance.

- Children's books are fun and funny or entertaining.
- They are colorful, visually appealing, artistic.
- Reading aloud provides opportunity for development of close, familial feelings or bonding; it is a positive family activity for both adults and children.
- Books build self-esteem in the child and adult.
- Children who are read to become better readers.
- Good children's books are not artificially contrived. They contain real everyday stories with universal morals and lessons.

- Books are culturally diverse. They provide opportunities to experience one's own or other cultures in positive ways.
- Children's books address almost every life problem or issue that children and families experience.
- They are nonthreatening because the stories are about animals or about children—not one's own.
- People at all levels of reading ability can use children's books, from nonreader (wordless books) on to advanced.
- Children's books are informational. Adults or children with limited skills can gain basic or specific information by reading them.
- Books teach and reinforce basic reading skills (left to right; prediction; main idea; use of picture clues; use of context; and so forth).
- Children's books provide *enjoyable* reading practice for children and adults.
- Bilingual and foreign language books are available.
- Children's books are readily available and *free* at the local public library.

INFORMATIONAL ASPECTS OF CHILDREN'S BOOKS

One important reason for using children's books with adult learners is that they contain valuable information written at a level that is easy to read and understand. Almost any subject can be found in the Juvenile or Young Adult collection of the public library as well as in the adult section. Even adults with good literacy skills often turn to children's books because difficult subjects like black holes or macroeconomics can be more easily understood from the simple text of a children's book.

Some topics commonly explored in children's books include:

- Emerging literacy skills: shapes, colors, ABCs, numbers, rhyme, vocabulary, sounds, visual discrimination, repetition
- Science
- Nutrition and Health
- Math
- Geography
- Language and Cultures (comparisons, slang, holidays, etc.)
- How things work
- Parenting issues such as discipline, siblings, self-esteem, school, addiction to drugs and alcohol

DISCUSSING PARENTING ISSUES

Parenting is often the most difficult issue for family literacy programs. Most librarians, tutors, and teachers do not necessarily consider themselves to be experts in parenting. Many of us learned a great deal as we raised our own children, but those experiences did not necessarily make us experts.

Family literacy programs often use guest speakers to stimulate discussions and introspection about parenting issues. Some of the topics presented for Santa Clara County Library's family literacy program include Safety In the Community, Stranger Danger, Safety in the Home, How to Enroll Your Child in School, How to Get Involved in Your Community, How to Get Involved in Your Child's Education, Stages in Child Development, Ways Different Cultures Care for Their Children, Balancing Love and Safety for Children, and Health and Your Children.

One effective way to deal with the issue of parenting in a family literacy program is to read children's books that directly or indirectly address the issue. Then facilitate discussion of the issues with groups of parents in your program. With this method, the staff or tutor need be only a skilled facilitator to guide the group, not necessarily a parenting expert.

There is no one right way to parent that all experts agree upon anyway. Facilitated group discussions that present the issue in the context of a book (rather than personal stories, which may be embarrassing or threatening) and then allow for a variety of opinions are very successful. This method also permits various cultural differences to enrich rather than inhibit the discussion.

The bibliography of children's books found in Appendix G contains short annotations concerning the different parenting issues explored in the books. Some of the ones typically requested by groups of parents include

- Discipline
- Siblings/sibling rivalry
- Illness/handicap/AIDS
- School/authority
- Death/loss
- Self-esteem
- Family/divorce
- Elderly people/aging
- Addiction: drugs, alcohol
- Incarceration

- Homelessness
- Ethnic experiences
- Love, making new friends, friendship

USING MAX AND RUBY TO INITIATE PARENTING DISCUSSIONS

Maria Salvadore, Head of Children's Services at the Martin Luther King Branch of D.C. Public Library, has been instrumental in introducing the concept of children's books as parenting tools. An enthusiastic and skilled storyteller, reader, and librarian, she has done much for the field of family literacy through her emphasis on the use of children's books for parenting. It was Maria who first convinced me to use children's books as the catalyst for parenting discussions.

One of my favorite books for demonstrating the ease with which a child's picture book can lead to discussions on a wide range of parenting issues is *Max's Chocolate Chicken* by Rosemary Wells. Although most author Well's books can be used this way, those in the Max and Ruby series are particularly effective because they are so easy to read yet portray realistic life situations.

With your group of parents and other adults read *Max's Chocolate Chicken* aloud. Usually I read the entire book myself, but sometimes I have each adult read a page (or one may pass if not comfortable with reading) as in the F.A.T.H.E.R.S. model. Since it is an easy book with a very limited vocabulary, both methods work. Be sure to either use a big book or to have one regular size copy for every two to three adults. It is important that all can see the illustrations clearly.

After reading the story, ask the parents a series of questions designed to lead them into discussions on a variety of parenting topics. Work from the premise that most adults already know a great deal more than they realize about developmental stages of children, typical sibling rivalry issues, and what they either want taught to their children or want to avoid teaching them. They may not be parenting experts, but these adults have all been children themselves, observed parents (both their own and others), and have a sense of what they want, or at least what they do not want, for the children in their lives.

These discussions built around children's books help the adults to think about their own parents and childhood, understand the degree of knowledge they already have, hear of others' experiences and opinions, and make better thought through and more informed choices for their own children.

Some of the questions that might be raised and discussed after reading *Max's Chocolate Chicken* include:

1. How old do you think Max is? Why do you think that?
2. How old do you think Ruby is? Why?
3. Is the game Max and Ruby play fair? Why or why not? Who set the rules? Are they fair? Why or why not?
4. How does Ruby treat Max? How does Max respond to Ruby? What does this say about the siblings? Is this typical?
5. Was Max wrong to steal the chicken and eat it? Why or why not?
6. Should Max have been punished?
   If yes, who should have punished him? What type of punishment?
   If no, what would be an appropriate parental response?
7. How had the "parent" rabbit prepared for this happening?
8. Is Max sorry in the end that he ate the chicken? Why do you say this?
9. Does Max love Ruby? Why do you think that?

No one ever said that being a parent was easy. This author would not propose to make parenting issues appear easy. But, they can be more comfortably and effectively addressed when using children's books as the catalyst for facilitated discussion. See Appendix A for a sample lesson from the F.A.T.H.E.R.S. program that uses children's books to initiate parenting discussion.

A PARENTING CURRICULUM FOR FAMILY LITERACY PROGRAMS

After the success of the F.A.T.H.E.R.S. curriculum at San Quentin, I decided that I wanted to develop that same basic concept for family literacy programs outside of a correctional setting. Jane Curtis and I developed a curriculum, initially for California's FFL programs, that can be used by libraries, Head Starts, schools, or in almost any situation where parenting issues need to be raised and discussed in a non-threatening environment.

Known as the P.A.R.E.N.T. S. (Parental Adults Reading, Encouraging, Nurturing, Teaching, Supporting) curriculum, a guide and training handbook were published and field tested in different settings in California in 1997 and 1998. Oakland Public Library was one of the field test sites. The FFL Coordinator there related that at the final parenting class in the P.A.R.E.N.T. S. series, one student said that the library's adult and family literacy program "is the only place where I feel comfortable and relaxed enough to share my experiences with other people who understand and are not judgmental."

The guide has been revised and is available from the California State Library Foundation. See Appendix A for a sample lesson from the guide.

NOTE

1. Jim Trelease. 1989. *The New Read Aloud Handbook*. New York: Penguin Books, 97.

9 FOLLOWING UP WITH EVALUATION

Without our program, I know of many families who would never have set foot in a public library to discover the services awaiting them. The first library orientation was a wash-out with only one family attending. At the suggestion of our director, I did not mention the library on the next invitation and all eligible families attended. Isn't it sad how those who need free public services the most are often the most intimidated by them!

—Deborah Salizzoni, former family literacy coordinator, Humboldt County (Calif.) Library

EVALUATING FAMILY LITERACY PROGRAMS

Evaluation is something everyone likes to talk about but no one likes to do! Maybe the reason so many people avoid evaluating their programs is their concern that a program they know to be successful at helping many people will not prove demonstrably effective in a formal evaluation.

Evaluation is just as important to a successful family literacy program, however, as are assessing needs and collaborating with partners. Without evaluation there is no accountability and without accountability it will be difficult, if not impossible, to find funding and support. Evaluation is a useful tool for refining and adjusting the program in order to make it more successful. Evaluation should not be viewed as punitive in nature but as a positive technique for improving the program.

Evaluation is the means by which program participants and others verify their success. Part of evaluation is the successful achievement of the goals and measurable objectives developed during the planning stages.

In a good program, evaluation begins with the planning stage and is ongoing throughout the life of the program. It is both formative in that it monitors the program as it moves toward its goals and summative in that it measures whether goals are met. In both cases, clear, definable, achievable objectives must be set at the beginning in order for evaluation to take place.

Evaluation should be both quantitative and qualitative. It may include surveys, such as the Parent Survey developed for FFL; logs and journals kept by both tutors and adult learners; individual interviews; focus group discussions and interviews; and expert opinions of outside evaluators.

One of the goals that makes family literacy programs difficult to evaluate is the improvement in the long-term literacy skills of the children. Most programs do not have the staff, funds, or time to conduct this sort of evaluation over a number of years. Even though this is clearly a goal, most programs will find they need to set shorter-term goals in regard to the children if they are to successfully evaluate.

In her ALA Fact Sheet on Evaluation of Family Literacy Programs, created as part of the Bell Atlantic-ALA Family Literacy Project, Debra Wilcox-Johnson gives a concise, two-page explanation of why and how to evaluate a family literacy program. She suggests that the library identify expected changes or accomplishments and select an appropriate method for evaluating them.

In another, unpublished document Dr. Wilcox-Johnson lists four major questions that you should consider when developing an evaluation plan.

1. Who and What to evaluate: for example, adult learners, tutors, program administration and design, materials, recruitment tools.
2. When to conduct the evaluation: formative needs to be ongoing while summative is more likely at the end.
3. Who to involve in the evaluation: everyone!
4. What changes do you want to see: for example, reading skills, reading habits, library usage, client satisfaction, continued funding.

A helpful guide for developing your own evaluation of a library-based literacy program can be found in *Evaluating Library Literacy Programs, A Manual for Reporting Accomplishments (1991)*. This manual was developed as the product of a 1990 LSCA Title VI grant to the State Library of New York.[1]

First and foremost your evaluation should reflect the mission and goals of your programs, both short and long term. It is also important that your program address the goals of the individual learners and the evaluation methods used should reflect these. Whenever possible, evaluation should focus on specified outcomes. In order to achieve all the above, it may be necessary to use different types of measurement.

CALIFORNIA'S FFL PARENT SURVEY

California's Families For Literacy programs have developed, over a number of years, a short evaluation tool that they have found very effective. The instrument is in the form of a survey that is given to the parent by the tutor at the beginning of their involvement in the family literacy program and annually thereafter.

It was clear from the beginning that the survey needed to be very

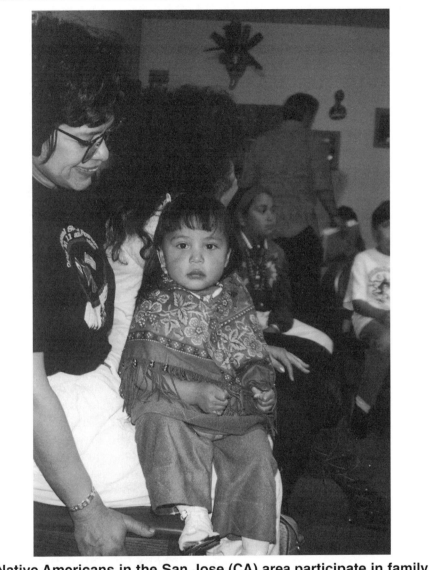

Native Americans in the San Jose (CA) area participate in family literacy activities at their local library. Evaluating their successes means addressing their cultural needs too.

short and easily administered. Both tutors and learners needed to know that the survey was to be useful to them in noting their own changes and successes, or it would be difficult to be sure they would complete the survey both at the beginning of the program and at the end of each year.

The original longer survey was broken into two parts, clearly separating the information on school-age children from preschoolers. In order to compress the survey into one two-sided sheet, these questions are no longer as clearly separated. The survey has evolved into what is now called *Families for Literacy Parent Survey*. The complete survey can be found in Appendix H.

The survey is not only used for evaluation but serves as a reminder to both tutors and learners of those goals toward which they want to strive for their children. It helps them focus from the beginning on things that are important in their lessons. Tutors and learners can refer to the survey throughout the year as a benchmark of the changes they and the children are experiencing.

OTHER EVALUATIVE MEASURES

Evaluation of adult literacy improvement can be done in a variety of ways. Many of California's library-based adult literacy programs in libraries use an instrument called CALPEP, the California Adult Learner Progress Evaluation Process. This was designed specifically for use with library learners. In addition, some libraries also use other more familiar instruments such as the BADER (named after the developer), CASAS (Comprehensive Adult Student Assessment System), TABE (Test of Adult Basic Education), and the LVA (Literacy Volunteers of America) assessment tools.

Increased use of library resources is one measure of success for family literacy participants. Other observable measures include the family's continued participation in program services, parent's involvement in children's school, improvements in parent's job or work status, and positive changes in the literacy environment in the home. Programs that use games, such as the Reading Challenge in Santa Clara County and the Reading Game in Oakland, also determine success by the number of games their families complete each series or each year.

Sutter County (Calif.) Library's Literacy Coordinator Mary Alice Shumate says that they measure success by how both adults and children share their activities at meetings and become more trusting. "Success is measured by FFL families who speak different languages (four) all laughing at the same time; doing the same activities and all appearing to enjoy it; hearing about children and all appearing to relate to the same parenting successes or difficulties."

Because all components can and should be improved, all components of a program should be evaluated. Even partners in the collaboration should evaluate their level of satisfaction with the partnership.

PORTFOLIO ASSESSMENTS

Portfolios are popular assessment tools in library-based literacy. These can be kept by the learner with the help and support of the tutor. Materials kept should include both the work of the family and the work of the adult learner alone.

Written work, photos, art, booklists, literacy games completed, news articles, completed craft activities related to storytimes or tutoring sessions, and any tests or evaluations should all become part of the portfolio. Tutor and learner should review the portfolio together periodically to jointly assess progress. The entire family should contribute to the portfolio and should occasionally review it together.

Direct quotes from tutors, learners, and children can be part of the portfolio. The following are some quotes taken from FFL program reports that might be used in a student's portfolio:

In May, our literacy coordinator made a presentation to our local battered women's support group. Seven-year-old José, a member of one of the recruited families, and his four-year-old brother were quite pleased at receiving books at the end of their first FFL class. The next week, however, Jose returned the books. I explained that the books were his to keep. He nodded his head and smiled. The next week he again tried to return the book. I told him, "You can keep this at home. You don't have to bring it back." He got very excited and repeated, "I can keep it? I can keep it?" He couldn't believe it! Turns out that he loves to read, and proved it by reading 32 books in one month.

Kathryn Bornhauser, FFL coordinator, Blanchard Community Library, Santa Paula, Calif.

Lupe came to the FFL program two years ago. She has worked well with her tutor and attended many programs with her son. Although unable to read and write in her native language, she is learning to read and write in English. Lupe was able to help us work with another parent in recruiting families to come for small group tutoring. Her ability to help increased her self-esteem, which had been very poor, and she now has gone on to a beginning ESL class and is also being tutored in reading and writing in Spanish by another FFL student.

Caroline Beverstock, adult literacy coordinator, San Mateo (Calif.) Public Library

Welfare reform is affecting many of our FFL clients. The Human Services Department placed one of our moms in a work experience position. Through a working partnership that included the student, her employer, the tutor, FFL coordinator, and the Human Services worker, a basic skills enhancement plan was developed. During the past four months, the student completed two reading books in the Challenger Series, two math books in Breakthrough to Math, and has added driver's license training to her plan. The student noted that her job duties are becoming easier as she is gaining additional skills. She is also able to take on additional responsibilities in her job.

Executive director, Siskiyou County's READ Project, Inc.

"The Families for Literacy program has made me more sure of myself, " said Ester. She has been in the tutoring program for over two years but had just started in the FFL program last year. Ester stated this while talking to one of the staff about how highly she thinks of the FFL program. "I am able to help out my daughter with her school work. Now my husband doesn't have to do it all."

Amy McHatten, FFL coordinator, Orange County Library

ANECDOTAL RECORDS AS EVALUATION

Although one should not rely totally on anecdotal records and information, they do provide valuable insight into the success of a program. Throughout this manual, quotations and anecdotes are used to enliven and make real the information contained here. For your program, too, these same techniques will be very useful.

The following is an anecdotal record written by Vi Christini, a family literacy aide at the Quartz Hill Branch of the County of Los Angeles Library's Families for Literacy Program. It tells the true literacy events in one man's life over a year in that program.

ONE YEAR IN THE LIFE OF A FAMILY LITERACY STUDENT

July: This month Michael was preparing for the birth of his daughter. She was born July 20th, and while admitting his wife [to the hospital], Michael said he had to have his wife read and sign all the papers because he couldn't. During this time his entire family was featured in the local newspaper, *Antelope Valley Press*. The photo and article were about family literacy. Michael is beginning in Laubach Book 2.

August: Michael was able to read a short story to his children. He said he was scared to death but at the same time enjoyed it so much.

September: Michael is now able to read many of the freeway off-ramp signs. He is also learning to read a map. Much of his work requires traveling. Often he lost valuable time because he would either get lost or have to ask directions.

October: Michael is not only reading to his three-year-old daughter but to the baby. Michael said, "I can't skip any pages while reading to the 3 year old because she knows the stories too well." According to his tutor he is progressing very rapidly in his workbook.

November: Michael never fails to mention that he spends as much time as possible reading to his children. His other children from his first marriage are all grown up now and he said he didn't even realize how important it was to be there to help with homework and reading. Now he has a grandson and Michael said, "I've already gotten him some books and read them to him."

December: [Michael] has started reading recipes and then preparing them for his family. Michael said he just loves doing this.

January: Michael's wife, Catherine, has just signed up in the literacy program and said her dream was to become a nurse. She is so impressed with Michael's progress and very proud of his efforts.

February: Michael reads the Sunday comics to his kids. He said he is reading everything he can. "I'm even reading the credits at the end of the movies," he said.

March: Michael is now able to leave notes at home and work. This is something that had always caused him a lot of frustration. Now he is able to write down information when someone is giving him directions, etc.

April: Michael is using a dictionary and said, "It's a wonderful feeling when I can find the word I'm looking for." He is working hard on improving his handwriting.

May: He is now able to help his eight-year-old son with his spelling tests and some of his homework. Michael said when Shawn needs help, I can say, "Let's go figure it out together."

June: Michael called to tell us he took his DMV (Department of Motor Vehicles) test and was able to read the entire test without any help. He missed only one question. He said he didn't think he could do it. Michael said, "This is a great feeling!" In the past he would have to have someone at the DMV office read the test for him. Michael said that was very embarrassing and he is so glad that he won't ever have to do it that way again.

July: Michael was telling me that last year when he looked around the library at the signs and poster he couldn't even attempt to read them. Now, however, he is able to read most of them without help. He said, "I don't call myself stupid or dumb anymore."

Children from Altadena (CA) Public Library succeed by reading their new books. They celebrate by thanking Huell Howser for helping their program to buy these important gift books.

A FINAL REALITY CHECK

Family literacy is the ultimate win-win service for libraries. Everyone gains when libraries take on the role of provider or partner in family literacy.

It is unrealistic, however, to expect the development or delivery of family literacy services to be without complications. Neither is it easy for the adults who need help to seek and successfully continue with literacy improvement for themselves and their families.

Nevertheless, do not be discouraged by the enormity of the problem nor the dedication required to found and fund a family literacy program in your community. Hundreds of libraries across the nation have already created and maintained successful programs. Hundreds of others have become valued partners in family literacy collaborations. It is time to make sure that in the future these numbers grow to thousands.

NOTE

1. *Evaluating Library Literacy Programs, A Manual for Reporting Accomplishments*, 1991. Albany: New York State Library.

AFTERWORD: HOW CAN LIBRARIES *NOT* BE INVOLVED?

Libraries are uniquely equipped to provide family literacy services. They are also good at doing what schools have not always been able to do—they can make reading and learning fun.

As an educator myself, I am only too aware of the differences in the way traditional education approaches reading and librarians approach reading. Few, if any, of us learned to *love* reading in school. We learned the skills of reading while attending our classes, but for many the joy of reading was experienced outside of a classroom. Teachers must adhere to rigid curriculum and standards. Librarians get to just share and enjoy good books with children. Both are needed as part of the literacy solution.

When family literacy programs exist, everyone wins. Research has shown that students who participate in preschool programs that involve parents have a greater high school graduation rate, a higher employment level, a lower adolescent pregnancy rate, and fewer special education placements. These trends not only result in a significant savings to the American taxpayer but make for a more economically secure and stronger individual, family, workplace, community, and nation.

The real question is not why or how can libraries provide family literacy. There are plenty of answers for that. The real question is how can libraries *not* be involved!

APPENDIX A

Sample Lessons from

F.A.T.H.E.R.S. Program

and

P.A.R.E.N.T.S. Curriculum Guide

F.A.T.H.E.R.S.

Fathers As Teachers: Helping, Encouraging, Reading, Supporting

PROGRAM GUIDE

by Jane Curtis

12. INCARCERATION & RECONNECTION

1. Incarceration is now a part of each inmates' family history. It is important to recognize and admit that incarceration really happened and removed the inmate from his family. Children's real loss must be heard and sympathized with.

2. Read together *Jafta: the Homecoming.* Point out that the loss Jafta feels is applicable to missing his father, no matter where he is. This book demonstrates the specialness of particular personal relationships. Note that the puppy grows as the story and the time progress.

3. Read together *When Andy's Father Went to Prison.* The book offers the child's point of view, illustrating issues specific to his father's being incarcerated. Andy's father's ability to articulate what his son is feeling is very powerful and brings Andy to tears with relief. This builds trust and is the basis for genuine reconnection.

4. Handout "How to Talk to Children About Your Incarceration." Ask each man to read one of the points on the page. Stop and reinforce the information by giving examples. When talking about doing "something bad," find language that makes sense to children. When drugs are involved, for example, suggest inmates talk about drug stores and Tylenol. They need to explain that *"people who make the rules for everyone decided that some drugs are not ok and that if you have them you will go to jail or prison."* This is a neutral description that provides information without creating confusion or instilling fear that if the child does not pick up his toys, he will go to prison.

5. Discuss talking to children who were present during arrest. Stress the importance of making the arrest real by providing an arena for communication and clarification of the event. Children doubt their own perceptions if they are not validated by at least one adult around them. Talk about what really happened so that confusion does not feed fearful or hostile fantasies. It is important that inmates try to establish the police as a resource for their children, not only as an enemy. Police should be described as having a job to do. If excessive force was used, then this, too, needs to be described and commented on without losing the information that police serve a function in society. This may lead to a discussion about how to do a good job at whatever you do.

6. Show books. *A Visit to the Big House* is the only other book found to deal with children of incarcerated fathers. It deals with the issues in a more superficial and less profound way. This is a good example of books on the same topic raising different awarenesses. *Boundless Grace* is the story of a black girl (about 10 or 11 years old) who has grown up with her mother and grandmother. Her father has never been part of her life, and he now lives in Africa with his wife and new family. He invites her to visit him there. The grandmother accompanies her, and the story addresses the feelings that Grace (from *Amazing Grace*) goes through about her father. The book's message is that "families are what you make them."

7. **Read to the class** *Papa and Me.* The humor in this book allows for distanced fathers to have a perspective on their attempts to connect or reconnect with their children. It encourages the men to keep reaching out and building memories for the future with their children.

Incarceration & Reconnection

PROCEDURE

WRITE ON BOARD
  Incarceration & Reconnection
  Tell class that incarceration is now part of
  their family history

OBJECTIVE

• indicate topic of lesson
• increase responsibility for each individual
  to break the cycle of incarceration

DISTRIBUTE BOOK
  Jafta: The Homecoming

READ ALOUD TOGETHER
• raise awareness of how children experience absence of a father

DISTRIBUTE BOOK
  When Andy's Father Went to Prison

READ ALOUD TOGETHER
• particularize loss to incarceration as part of
  family history

Incarceration & Reconnection – Continued

PROCEDURE	OBJECTIVE

HANDOUT
   "How to Talk to Children About Your Incarceration"
READ TOGETHER as a class
DISCUSS
   If children were present at inmate's arrest, he must talk to them about what happened and follow the guidelines on the handout
	• raise awareness of children's reality and how to help them process their concerns
	
	• help children process traumatic experiences so they will not be drawn to repeat the cycle from lack of information

SHOW BOOK A Visit to the Big House	• broaden awareness of scarcity of books available on topic of an incarcerated father
SHOW BOOK Boundless Grace	• expose class to book about reconnection
READ ALOUD TO CLASS Papa and Me	• show that sometimes connecting with children is a bumpy road and does not go as planned • demonstrate the need for love, patience, time and a sense of humor

P.A.R.E.N.T.S.

Parental Adults Reading, Encouraging, Nurturing, Teaching, Supporting

by
Jane Curtis, M.A.

with
Dr. Carole Talan,
Family Literacy Specialist

CURRICULUM GUIDE

4. LANGUAGE ACQUISITION: REASONS FOR RHYME

1. The importance of language. Discuss with learner/s why language is important—communication, self-expression, literacy, information. Without language, an individual's world is limited. The deaf develop a language of their own, i.e., sign language. In order to interact with others we all develop language.

2. Language acquisition continuum. Language is not learned all at once, it is acquired over time. Listening, speaking, reading, and writing proceed developmentally.

Our listening vocabulary is much greater than our speaking vocabulary, especially when young. It is good and important to read books to children where the language is more advanced than what they are able to say. This is one way to build vocabulary. Point out that both listening and reading are receptive, while speaking and writing are active and generative.

For many of us writing is the most difficult, even more difficult than reading. Writing is one aspect of language which adults continue to develop because it is the most challenging.

3. What parents can do to promote language development in children. For each aspect on the continuum, ask learner/s to respond with specific behaviors.

To develop listening skills: talk to children; read to them (the same book over and over, if they want); name objects; describe in full sentences what you are doing, what they are doing, what is going on in the environment.

To develop speaking skills: ask children to tell you about their day; listen to how they feel and what they think; read to them and ask them to answer questions about the story and the pictures.

To develop reading skills: read to children and with them; listen to them read; ask them to read notes, messages and signs; help them with reading homework. Make games of reading signs, billboards, posters and other items they see in their environment.

To develop writing skills: encourage drawing, scribbling and copying; write down the words they use to describe the pictures they are drawing; write lists and messages; ask them to write their names and to leave you notes and write letters. Keep a family journal to which both adult and child can contribute.

4. Learning to read in your first language. It is difficult to first learn to read a language that one does not hear spoken at home. There are, however, English/Spanish books for Latino children learning to read English as their second language, such as *My First 100 Words in Spanish & English, My Day/Mi Dia, Margaret and Margarita.* Bilingual books in other languages are available but not with as much variety as those in Spanish.

Help learner/s who speak a language other than English in their home to value their first language. Encourage them to help their children read and write in both English and their first language. It is a tremendous asset in the job market to be truly bilingual.

In some families, children may be more proficient at reading English than parents. They can share a book by taking turns, the parent supplying the native vocabulary while the child reads the English words.

Remind learner/s that the best learning environment is often one where both adult and child, teacher and student, are learning together. With this in mind, the parent can develop the respect of the more English proficient child by valuing the adult's commitment to continue learning. They can also discuss the kind of encouragement and support from teachers and family members each likes to have in order to be successful learners.

5. Read to learner/s *Is Your Mama a Llama?* Allow learner/s to listen to and experience the effects of rhyme before you ask them to understand its importance. Get into the rhythm and expressiveness of the book. Stop in strategic places and allow learner/s to call out the next word, the "answer." Show how easy it is to be right. We all like to know the right answer, but emphasize how important it is for children to have many opportunities to be right in order to build their self-esteem.

6. The importance of rhyme. Ask learner/s to generate a list of why so many books for young children contain rhymes. Be sure to include that rhyme is *predictable,* so it helps *build success* and thereby increases *self-esteem* in children.

Rhyme is repetitive, rhythmic and fun, and invites *participation,* thereby utilizing the kinesthetic learning channel. Because it is fun and easy to be successful, rhyme helps children remember new words and their meanings, so it is excellent for *memory development.*

Ask learner/s to recite rhymes remembered from childhood. Take this opportunity to share cross-culturally. Childhood rhymes are usually still remembered because they came in through a window of opportunity (from video *"Your Child's Brain"*) when language was first learned and repetition was extremely effective.

7. Read aloud together *Goodnight Moon.* Introduce the book as a classic first published in 1947. Demonstrate the many ways to use the book for language development, e.g., point out object names, repeat the "goodnight" phrase while naming other objects, find the mouse in each color picture, describe changes in the light, the moon, the clocks, etc.

8. Show other rhyming books: *The Alphabet Tale; Mother Hubbard's Cupboard; Big Owl Little Towel; Where's My Teddy?; Ten, Nine, Eight; A Fox Got My Sox; Pink, Red, Blue, What Are You?* Read as many as you have time for, encouraging learner/s to contribute the next word.

9. Read aloud together *Leo the Late Bloomer.* Children develop at different rates and it is important to be supportive and encouraging of children while trusting the process of growth.

Discuss how this book can be used to open a conversation about feeling slow or different, how it offers the opportunity to explain figures of speech and common sayings (late bloomer, a watched pot never boils). Other books with a playful approach to language: *The King Who Rained, A Little Pigeon Toad, Rib Ticklers.*

Language Acquisition: Reasons for Rhyme

PROCEDURE	OBJECTIVE
WRITE ON BOARD OR IN NOTEBOOK Language Acquisition: Reasons for Rhyme	• indicate topic of lesson
ASK LEARNER/S Why is learning language important? What is language good for?	• understand without language there is no literacy for written communication and self-expression
WRITE ON BOARD OR IN NOTEBOOK "Language Acquisition" continuum in list format with vertical arrow going from top to bottom: • listening • speaking • reading • writing	• teach that learning language and becoming literate evolves over time and is a process that involves child's interaction with the environment
WRITE ON BOARD OR IN NOTEBOOK next to Language Acquisition: "What parents can do" Create a list that corresponds to what child does as s/he acquires language • talk and read aloud (listening) • ask questions and listen with real interest (speaking) • point out letters, signs, words, share books, listen to reading without much correction (reading) • ask for drawings, notes, messages taken, make lists, write letters (writing)	• show how parental involvement can support and promote acquisition of language and development of literacy in specific, easy to do, concrete ways

SHOW BOOKS
Spanish/English books
   My 1st 100 Words in Sp/Eng
   My Day/Mi Dia
   Margaret and Margarita
	• understand it is best to learn to read in the language heard the most, your first language
	• understand that being bilingual is a tremendous asset in the job market

Language Acquisition: Reasons for Rhyme – Continued

PROCEDURE

UNDERLINE ON BOARD OR IN NOTEBOOK
  Reasons for Rhyme

READ BOOK TO LEARNER/S
  Is Your Mama a Llama?

ASK LEARNER/S
  What good is rhyme, what does it offer?
  1) it is PREDICTABLE
  2) it encourages PARTICIPATION
  3) it develops MEMORY
  4) it builds SUCCESS and SELF-ESTEEM
  5) it is repetitive and rhythmic
ASK for rhymes remembered from childhood

OBJECTIVE

- indicate next topic area
- demonstrate how rhyme enables participation and successful guessing
- understand the value of rhyme and why so many children's books use it
- refer to ABC video's claim that repetition and singing and rhyme are most effective for brain development in young children
- show how what is learned at an early age this way is retained for long periods
- provide opportunity for cross-cultural sharing

DISTRIBUTE BOOK
  Goodnight Moon
READ ALOUD TOGETHER
- show that repetitiveness and rhythm make this book a classic (1st published in 1947)
ASK for location of mouse on each color page and any other changes noticed
- involve learners in details of book
SHOW BOOKS
  Mother Hubbard's Cupboard
  Pink, Red, Blue...
  Big Owl Little Towel
  Alphabet Tale
  A Fox Got My Sox
  Where's My Teddy?
  10, 9, 8

- show predominance of rhyme and how easy it is to get involved and guess what comes next

DISTRIBUTE BOOK
  Leo the Late Bloomer
READ ALOUD TOGETHER
- show the importance of developmental timing, appropriate expectations, self-esteem, and how book offers an opportunity to talk with child about feelings and self-esteem

APPENDIX B

Bibliography of Easy-to-Read Parenting Books

Bibliography of Easy to Read Parenting Books
(Developed for Families for Literacy Programs)

Title	Author or Publisher	ISBN
As a Child Grows	Rosanne Keller	0883365111
		0883365545 (Spanish)
The Childbearing Year	Barbara B. Holstein	0883365677
A Good Beginning: Enjoying Your Baby's First Year	Barbara S. Lewis	0883365707
		0883365529 (Spanish)
Having a Baby	New Readers Press	0568530323
Let's Work It Out Series	New Readers Press	
Seven titles at reading levels 2–3		0–883362821
Seven titles at reading levels 4–6		0–88336283X
Preschool Games and Activities	Sandra Taetzsch	0822456052
The Safe, Self-Confident Child	New Readers Press	1568530374
Teen Pregnancy: Why Are Kids Having Kids	L. Rosakis	0805025693
When a Baby Is New	Rosanne Keller	0883365170
		0883365537 (Spanish)
You and Your Child's Teacher	Pamela Weinberg	0883366274
Your Home Is a Learning Place	Pamela Weinberg	088336641X

More Difficult Reading But Worth Using with Adult New Readers:

Title	Author or Publisher	ISBN
How to Talk So Kids Can Learn at Home and in School	Adele Faber and Elaine Maylish	068482728
How to Talk So Kids Will Listen & So Kids Will Talk	Adele Faber and Elaine Maylish	0684813335
It's Perfectly Normal	Robie Harris	1564021998
The Parent's Handbook: Systematic Training for Effective Parenting	Dinkmeyer, Don, Sr., McKay, Gary, and Don Dinkmeyer, Jr	679777989
Parenting Young Children: Systematic Training for Effective Parenting of Children under Six	Dinkmeyer, Don, Sr., Don Dinkmeyer Sr., Gary McKay, James S. Dinkmeyer, and Don Dinkmeyer Jr.	0785411895
Without Spanking or Spoiling	Elizabeth Crary	943990742

APPENDIX C

Sample Memorandum of Agreement

APPENDIX C
SAMPLE MEMORANDUM
OF AGREEMENT

This agreement is between the Heavenly Valley Head Start Center (Head Start) and the Heavenly Valley Public Library (Library) regarding special programs and related materials and services to be provided by the Library for the benefit of Head Start children, parents, and teachers.

ADMINISTRATION
The Library hereby designates _____, a member of its staff, as its liaison to Head Start for purposes of administering this agreement.

Head Start hereby designates _____, a member of its staff, as its liaison to the Library for purposes of administering this agreement.

Any change, amendment to, or other variation from this agreement shall be in writing and duly signed by authorized representatives of the parties.

Any dispute arising between the parties during the course of the agreement, if it cannot be resolved informally, shall be decided by arbitration. Each party shall appoint an arbitrator who together shall select a third arbitrator to serve on an arbitration panel. The dispute shall be resolved by the panel under the rules of the American Arbitration Association, with a majority of two votes necessary for resolution.

This agreement may be cancelled by either party upon _____ days written notice to the other party.

TERM OF AGREEMENT
The term of this agreement is from October 1, 1997 to September 30, 1998.

LIBRARY SERVICES AND MATERIALS
The Library shall, at reasonable times to be agreed upon by the parties:

1. Provide four (4) _____ focused programs, each lasting approximately _____ hours for children at Head Start's site. (this could be literacy, nutrition, safety, etc.)
   (Attachment A, incorporated herein by reference, is a description of the programs.)

2. Provide one (1) literacy/library focused program for Head Start parents at Head Start's site lasting approximately _____ hours.
(Attachment B, incorporated herein by reference, is a description of the program.)

3. Provide one (1) library/literacy focused program for Head Start teachers, parents, and children at library's site lasting approximately _____ hours.
(Attachment C, incorporated herein by reference, is a description of the program.)

4. Provide special, long term book loan arrangements for Head Start sites and families.

5. Provide one (1) special orientation program at the Library for Head Start teachers in family literacy and the related use of library resources.
(Attachment D, incorporated herein by reference, is a description of the program.)

6. Provide library consulting services for Head Start Teachers not to exceed _____ hours in book selection for Head Start classes, and to assist Head Start in expanding on books/topics used in its program.

7. Provide tutoring services as applicable for Head Start parents in need of literacy.
(N.B. If the library does not provide literacy tutoring services, it could provide help with referral to tutoring services instead.)

8. Provide special notice and invitation to Head Start classes and families concerning regular library activities for children which would be applicable to the children's ages and interests, such as storytimes, special children's programs, etc.

9. Provide books and materials to Head Start children, parents, and teachers as set forth in Attachment E, which is hereby incorporated by reference.

HEAD START SERVICES AND MATERIALS
Head Start shall, at reasonable times to be agreed upon by the parties:

1. Provide transportation for Head Start children, teachers and parents to a minimum of two (2) programs at the library site.

2. Provide transportation occasionally and as necessary for Head Start children to the library to check out books on a regular schedule to be agreed upon by the parties.

3. Reimburse the Library for books and other materials specified in Attachment E. (Average of $3 per book, 5 books per child, 20 children per class, 4 programs plus 1 parent meeting and one classroom set of the same books per year.)

4. Provide two to four volunteers to be trained by library staff to assist with the Head Start library program.

5. Provide a set, dedicated, and agreed upon time for the programs specified herein with no other activities scheduled that would interfere with the programs.

6. Childcare while parents receive literacy tutoring (if literacy tutoring is provided).

PAYMENT
Head Start shall pay the Library a total of $_____ for the services and materials specified herein as more specifically set forth in Schedule 1, attached hereto and incorporated herein by reference. (Optional) Payment of $_____ monthly in arrears shall be made to the Library by Head Start upon receipt of a duly executed monthly invoice from the Library.

FEDERAL FUND REQUIREMENTS APPLICABLE
All federal regulations pertaining to equal employment opportunity, wages, nondiscrimination in employment, and other requirements found in the Code of Federal Regulations with respect to recipients of federal funds are applicable. Attached hereto and incorporated by reference are the provisions applicable to this agreement, which the Library hereby agrees to.

Dated: September 8, 1997

Signed:

_____   _____
Director, Heavenly Valley   Director, Heavenly Valley
Public Library   Head Start Center

APPENDIX D

Leading Your Child to Reading

APPENDIX D
LEADING YOUR CHILD
TO READING

(You can use these 18 points below to develop a handout for use with adult new readers. For best results, design the handout using a large, easy-to-read font. It is not necessarily self-explanatory, however, but should be discussed first in a group situation to allow the adults an opportunity to explore the significance of each step to their child's language and literacy development and to be sure they understand the concept.)

1. **Talk** to and with your child.

2. **Listen** to your child and encourage his/her listening.

3. **Share** at least one book everyday with your child. You do not have to be able to read to share a book with your child!

4. Select a quiet, comfortable place to share a book with your child. Before bed or nap time is good.

5. Make reading times **fun**, a family ritual. Allow for the age and needs of your child. If it's not fun, don't do it!

6. Share stories from your life, family, work, etc., and have your child share stories of his/her daily life with you.

7. Your child is **never too young** to be read to! Start when your child is still an infant. Start even when still pregnant. Even before they are born, babies respond to sound and language.

8. It is OK, even good, to read the same book/story over and over to a child. Children love to hear books repeated many times. Do not be upset if your child tries to turn the pages or talks while you are reading. This is not bad. Children, especially young ones, often need to touch the book, even put it in their mouths, and to be active while being read to. It may take time for your child to learn to sit still and enjoy being read to. Please be patient.

9. You don't have to read every word in a book to share it with your child.

10. Children need to see reading as a **fun** thing to do if they are to become good readers, and the school doesn't always make reading fun. That is your job.

11. Use every reading opportunity that you can with your child. Point out at least one beautiful (interesting, unusual) thing everyday and help your child to use his/her imagination.

12. **Think and talk** about the story (stories) that you read as you go about your daily life.

13. Remember, even when your children can read, they still need to be read to! Even adults enjoy being read to.

14. Encourage remembering, imaging, fantasizing and share these.

15. Young children need to **hear** language. It can be spoken, read, sung. They need to **play** with words and rhymes and songs. Music is wonderful and your child will love to listen and sing with you.

16. In order to learn a second language, children must hear **that** language. Babies learn by listening. You should be proud of your first language, but help your child to hear English so that he/she will learn to speak and read it.

17. Remember, a child's work is his play; therefore **play** is an essential part of the child's life and he needs to play every day. Children learn much about their life and their world through their play.

18. Take your child to the **library**. Have the librarian help you pick out books your child will enjoy. Remember, all the books in the library are **free**. But, you must remember to return them too!

Dr. Carole Talan, State Literacy Resource Center of California
December, 1998

APPENDIX E

Sample Family Literacy
Tutor Training Agendas

APPENDIX E
SAMPLE FAMILY
LITERACY TUTOR
TRAINING AGENDAS

TRAINING THE FAMILIES FOR LITERACY (FFL) TUTOR
Provided by Jane Curtis at the FFL Symposium. December 9, 1995

I. INTRODUCTION

The FFL experience defined/explained

II. WHO IS THE FFL TUTOR?

1. It is hard to find good FFL tutors.

2. Family literacy training should be integrated into regular tutor training and given to all prospective tutors.

3. It is essential that FFL tutors have experience with children.

III. TRAINING PHILOSOPHY

1. Learn through repetition and by creating a framework on which the tutors can "hang" new information.

2. As a group, identify all areas of contact with prospective FFL tutors (phone, orientation, tours, etc.).

3. Introduce family literacy at tutor orientation and within the regular training received by all tutors. Focus on family literacy in additional training for FFL tutors and in periodic inservices/support groups for tutors.

IV. DEFINE TUTOR ROLE

1. Critical key concepts often need regular repetition

    a) Improve parents' literacy skills through reading aloud children's books to children.

b) Tutor does NOT teach the child to read but may help parent teach child to read and to do homework.

2. Reading aloud and using books to stimulate preliteracy activities (pointing to objects, naming objects, identifying colors, shapes, counting) and to promote conversation

V. PROGRAM GOALS AND FAMILY LITERACY

1. Family literacy components

   a) adult literacy skills

   b) emerging literacy needs of child

   c) family activities around books and reading

   d) parenting skills

2. It is important to spell out your goals so that tutors will understand and embrace them and know what to do and why

   a) Empower parents as their child's first teacher.

   b) Encourage and enable adult learners to read aloud to their children on a regular basis.

   c) Promote a love of reading as an activity to be enjoyed by the whole family.

   d) Develop parents' literacy skills of verbal communication, reading and writing by using preschool materials of interest to their children.

   e) Introduce and welcome families to the public library and educate them to the resources available there.

   f) Provide each family with free high-quality children's literature for their home library.

VI. CHILD DEVELOPMENT/LANGUAGE ACQUISITION

1. What tutors need to know so that they can help parents become effective as their child's first teacher.

a) how children learn to read

b) how preliteracy activities build foundation for reading

c) age appropriate books and how to use them.

2. How to give tutors information on child development that they need

a) Show videos such as *Read Aloud Now!* and *From Crib to Classroom.*

b) Hands-on activities (Have tutors do with each other what parent is to do with child.)

VII. FFL TRAINING BOOK ACTIVITY

1. Divide into groups of 3–5 people.

2. Distribute children's books to each group.

3. Each group reads book and addresses questions:

a) This book is appropriate for what age child?

b) This book is appropriate for what level adult learner?

c) What specific reading/language skills can be taught with this book?

4. Small groups report back to large group.

5. Group discussion of the activity.

VIII. FFL TUTOR SUPPORT SERVICES

1. Mark family literacy books in library with smiley stickers on spine

2. Gift books for tutors to choose for use in lessons

3. Book/activity packets to use as lesson plans

4. Activities with resource books

IX. GIFT BOOK COLLECTION

1. List of suggested books

2. How to choose children's books

3. How to teach parents/adults to choose children's books

HUNTINGTON BEACH PUBLIC LIBRARY'S FAMILY LITERACY TUTOR TRAINING OUTLINE
Amy Crepeau, FFL (Families for Literacy) Coordinator

SESSION I (ONE HOUR)

Overview of the Family Literacy Program

Goals of the Family Literacy Program

View and discuss California Literacy Campaign's Families for Literacy Video (15 min.)

Homework assignment for Session II: Read "If You Can Read This, Thank Your Parents" a newspaper article from the *Orange County Register*. September 8, 1995.

SESSION II (TWO HOURS)

Tour of Children's Department at Central Library

Overview of types of children's books available for families to read together and books that may appeal to adult learners in the children's section.

Preschool storytime at the library (we sit in on a lapsit storytime to see types of books, songs, and techniques that appeal to preschoolers)

Using children's books with adults (I use a lot of ideas and handouts)

Why use children's books with adults / Instructional features of children's book

How to choose books for your learner's reading level and age of child, and How to reinforce skills in the lesson. (I make a display of types of books for different adult reading levels and ages of children, and I give tutors the Family Literacy Bibliography for Adult Learners)

How to make reading with adult learners easier (tips for picking books that won't intimidate your learner)

Do's and Don'ts when using children's books

Demonstration of how to plan a lesson around a children's book. (I usually use *The Very Hungry Caterpillar* or *Hooray For Snail)*

Pair or Small Group practice—choose a children's book and decide what level adult student it would be helpful for, what age child might enjoy the book, and what elements tutors see in the book that might be useful for an adult learner (possible sight words, word patterns, important vocabulary/grammar concepts, discussion topics). We sometimes run short of time and do this segment in Session III.

Homework—review "Getting Your Children Ready to Read" and "Reading Aloud" (handouts)

SESSION III (ONE HOUR)

Tour of local library with an emphasis on how to find children's books in the library and literacy collection.

**CONTRA COSTA COUNTY LIBRARY'S PROJECT
SECOND CHANCE (PSC)
Agenda for Families for Literacy Component
of Tutor Training
(55 minutes)**

1.   INTRODUCTION/NEEDS/GOALS

Many of the adult learners in Project Second Chance have young children. FFL works with those adult learners and their children. This component of the program is funded by a grant from the California State Library. We know that illiteracy breeds illiteracy. If the parent doesn't read, chances are the children don't read; no books in the home, no one to model the importance of reading.

FFL attempts to interrupt this cycle by making family literacy part of the one-on-one tutoring session. Emphasis of this program is on the parent as the teacher. The tutor works with the adult learner; the learner goes home and works with his/her children. FFL works with adult learners with children age four or under.

The goals of FFL are to

- introduce quality children's literature
- establish home libraries by giving books to the families
- equip parents with the skills to prepare children for reading
- create library users
- build self-esteem—kids don't live in a vacuum
- model the joy and value of reading

2.   WHAT YOU AS A TUTOR CAN DO

Reading to children is the easiest way to assure their academic success. See the attached handout, "Literacy Development in Young Children," listing the ways reading can influence the learning process. As a PSC tutor of an adult learner in the FFL program, you will be reading children's books with your adult learner as part of your lesson, so the learner can, in turn, read them to their children. Impress on the learner how simple this activity is once they feel comfortable with the books.

In addition to reading children's material in your one-on-one tutoring session, FFL tutors are requested to

- attend PSC family storytimes with your learner and his or her children,
- attend at least one in-library event, and
- arrange for a tour of learner's local library during first six months

and point out children's area, where to check out books, how to get a library card.

If you are matched with an FFL learner, you will receive, upon being matched, an "FFL Tutor Handbook." Read this. You will also receive your first packet of materials to introduce to your learner. It will include age-appropriate books to get you started plus notices of upcoming library events at learner's local library and a children's magazine such as *Babybug*, *Ladybug*, or *Spider*.

Begin by reviewing page 13 of your tutor manual, "Why Read to Your Child," with your adult learner.

3.   FILLING OUT YOUR DATA SHEET

PSC will honor preferences you have for an adult learner. If you indicate on your data sheet that you are interested in FFL, then you will probably be assigned an adult learner who is part of this program as a parent-to-be, parent, grandparent with primary care, or a daycare provider of children age five years or under.

4.   BIRTHDAY BOOKS

All children, aged 0–12 years, of PSC learners receive cards announcing that a birthday book (age appropriate) will be waiting for them at their nearest library when their birthday months roll around. To obtain this information, birthdates (day, month, and year) are noted when learner is first interviewed on intake or when the tutor does an informal interest inventory. There is space on each of these forms for this information.

5.   THE FUN PART

We're going to take some time today to read children's books. First I am going to read you a story, then ask you some questions about what I have just read

Now, I want you to work with a partner, one of you will be the tutor, the other the learner. After five minutes, switch. Spend sometime looking at the book, then duet read, echo read, or model read. Talk about the book; ask questions that can't be answered with just a "yes" or "no."

6.   WHAT PSC WILL DO FOR YOU

I will be in touch with you on a regular basis. Call me anytime with questions, requests or concerns. The PSC staff works together to meet your needs and those of the adult learners. Interaction with you is very important to us.

CONCLUSION

We can help break the cycle of illiteracy by giving adult learners the necessary tools to work with their preschool children. This can be done by adults with low literacy skills and you will see what a difference this combined effort of teaching them and empowering them to teach their children will make in their lives.

APPENDIX F

Sample Materials for Tutor Manuals

APPENDIX F
SAMPLE MATERIALS FOR TUTOR MANUALS

TABLE OF CONTENTS
Contra Costa County Library's Families For Literacy Tutor Manual

Family Literacy
Parent Survey
FFL Packets
Baby Materials
Family Events
Creating Library Users
Monthly Calendar
Project Second Chance Newsletter
Birthday Books
Parenting Materials
FFL Children's Book List
Assisting the New Reader in the Children's Library
Tutor and Adult Learners—Reviewing Picture Books
Materials to Use with the Adult Learner:
   Why Read to Children
   Hints for Reading to Your Child
   More Tips on How to Read to Your Child
   Getting Your Child Ready to Read
   More Ideas for Getting Your Child Ready to Read
   Different Books for Different Ages
   Books for Toddlers
   Ideas for Using Word Cards
   What Children Learn and What Parents Can Do to Help
   Beginning Writing
   Caring Acts for Busy Parents
   Parenting: The Importance of Good Communication
   Reading Ideas
   Kindergarten Readiness
   Your and Your Child's School
   Communicating with the Teacher
   Homework Tips
   Oh No! I've Got a Test!

Created by Beth Bochser, Contra Costa County (CA) Library's
Project Second Chance, for her Families for Literacy Tutor Manuals
925–927–3250

LITERACY DEVELOPMENT IN YOUNG CHILDREN

Reading to children is the single most important thing that you can do to assure their academic success. Start reading to children at birth and never stop.

Reading to children builds

COORDINATION by
  focusing eyes
  coordinating mind and muscles
  handling books

ORDER by
  establishing the book format; beginning, middle, end
  developing sequential order and logic

CONCENTRATION by
  remembering the sequence of events
  sitting for extended periods in preparation for school
  understanding much more than children can express

VISUAL DISCRIMINATION by
  identifying colors and shapes
  making the connections between two- and three-dimensional objects
  noticing details
  building imagination

LANGUAGE DEVELOPMENT by
  hearing different sounds
  hearing the rhythm of language
  developing vocabulary and sentence structure
  hearing words used in a meaningful context
  developing self-expression
  becoming familiar with the question and answer format
  exposing children to material beyond their reading level

READING READINESS by
  realizing that words are written down
  using familiar refrains and rhymes as first readers
  developing the connection between reading and writing

ACTIVE LISTENING by
  developing the ability to make predictions
  gathering information
  exposing children to a variety of environments and situations
  developing deductive thinking

INDEPENDENCE by
  promoting ownership of books
  seating at story time
  choosing own reading material
  presenting an externalized way of dealing with inner fears

SOCIALIZATION by
  communicating
  interacting between reader and audience
  relaying values

SELF-ESTEEM by
  developing a positive attitude toward reading
  encouraging independence
  increasing time spent with children
  encouraging relationship with parents and providers
  seeing self in books

Created by Beth Bochser, Contra Costa County (CA) Library's Project Second Chance, for her Families for Literacy Tutor Manuals 925–927–3250

GETTING YOUR CHILD READY TO READ

1. Ask questions and answer your child's questions.

   (A child who asks questions is ready to learn.)

2. Read everything: labels, recipes, cereal boxes, comic strips, signs.

   (Let your child see you read.)

3. Talk to your child. Listen to your child.

   (Help build self-esteem and vocabulary.)

4. Have books, magazines, and newspapers in your home.

   (Make reading a part of your and your child's lives.)

5. Make learning fun.

   Enjoy your child and your child's way of learning.

Created by Beth Bochser, Contra Costa County (CA) Library's Project Second Chance, for her Families for Literacy Tutor Manuals 925–927–3250

DIFFERENT BOOKS FOR DIFFERENT AGES

Birth to one year:
   sing lullabies and songs
   picture books should be clear, bright, simple
   one or two pictures per page makes it easier for baby to focus
   board or plastic books with easy to turn pages

One to two years:
   introduce clapping rhymes and knee bounces
   wordless and word list books
   simple "good night" books
   sturdy, feely, scent and squeaky books

Two to three years:
   stories that repeat catchy phrases
   sturdy pop-up and pull-tab books
   short stories with few words and many pictures
   ABC, counting, color and shape books

Three to five years:
   introduce non-fiction; dinosaurs, trucks, farm animals
   simple folktales
   longer stories and more detailed pictures
   let child choose books of interest to him/her
   stories that can be acted out

Beginning readers:
   short stories; few words per page; pictures that match text
   books that interest child
   real life stories, simple biographies
   joke and riddle books
   simple magazines

Continue reading to your child after he/she begins to read. Choose books at a somewhat higher reading level than your child's. Try reading chapter books, reading one chapter every evening.

Created by Beth Bochser, Contra Costa County (CA) Library's Project Second Chance, for her Families for Literacy Tutor Manuals 925–927–3250

HINTS FOR READING TO YOUR CHILD

1. Read the book to yourself first.

2. Pick a time when your child is calm.
   Try the same time each day.

3. Find a comfortable and quiet place away from the T.V. and phone.

4. Let your child sit close to you or on your lap.

5. Make this a fun time. Enjoy the story and your child.
   Ask questions about the pictures and the story.
   Let your child ask questions too.

6. Try making your voice get loud, soft, fast, and slow to make the story interesting.

7. If your child gets bored or fussy, try a different book or a different time.

Created by Beth Bochser, Contra Costa County (CA) Library's Project Second Chance for her Families for Literacy Tutor Manuals 925–927–3250

TALKING TO YOUR CHILD

HOW?

Sit down and really listen to your child.

Be honest with your child.

It is okay to disagree with your child.

It is okay to say "I don't know" to your child.

WHEN?

In the car

Walking to school

Cooking dinner

Waiting at the doctor's

At bedtime

While watching TV

WHAT ABOUT?

What makes you mad?

What are your favorite foods?

If you could go anywhere. . . . ?

How would you feel if. . . . ?

What did you do at school. . . . ?

What do you think about. . . . ?

Created by Beth Bochser, Contra Costa County (CA) Library's Project Second Chance, for her Families for Literacy Tutor Manuals 925–927–3250

COMMUNICATING WITH THE TEACHER

Sometimes you will need to write notes to your child's teacher to explain your child's absence or to respond to a note from the teacher

Always include: date
                              greeting
                              child's name
                              date of absence
                              reason for absence
                              closing
                              your signature

SAMPLE NOTE: _____

September 20, 1999

Dear Mrs. Smith,

My daughter, Angela Morits, was absent on September 18 because she had a fever and a sore throat.

Sincerely,

_____

If your want the teacher to call you, give the teacher a phone number and a time that she can reach you. Remember that it may be hard for a teacher to make calls during the school day.

If you want to meet with the teacher, give the teacher days and times that you can meet with her.

When talking with her:
  be on time for the meeting
  plan what you want to say ahead
  listen carefully
  keep an open mind
  think about what is best for your child

Adapted from materials created by Beth Bochser, Contra Costa County (CA) Library's Project Second Chance, for her Families for Literacy Tutor Manuals
925–927–3250

BEGINNING WRITING
Being able to write a word will help a child to read that word.

1. Writing muscles are developed by doing many things: buttoning, zipping, and tying shoes; using eating utensils and scissors; playing with clay.

2. Have materials for writing: crayons, pencils, markers, chalk, chalkboard, lined, and unlined paper. Also, try writing in sand, salt, and shaving cream.

3. Let your children see you write grocery lists, telephone messages, directions. Read aloud as you write. This shows your children that reading and writing are connected.

4. Children learn to write by writing. Scribbles lead to writing.

5. Display your children's writing. Be a proud parent.

6. Find good things to say about your child's writing. Show that you care.

When Your Children Are Ready To Write Letters And Words:

1. Teach your children to write in the style used by your local schools.

2. When children first write they may mix up letters and combine words; don't worry, this is normal.

3. Getting started:
    Have children trace letters with their fingers before writing.
    Draw a circle, a cross and a square and have your children copy them.
    Let your children trace letters and words. Try writing words with a yellow marker and have your children write over it in a darker color.
    When children copy words, draw lines for them to write on.

Writing Ideas for Children:
1. Make greeting cards and bookmarks.
2. Staple blank papers together for children to use as letter and word booklets.
3. Have children sign their artwork, letters, and notes to the family.

Created by Beth Bochser, Contra Costa County (CA) Library's Project Second Chance, for her Families for Literacy Tutor Manuals 925–927–3250

HOMEWORK TIPS

- Ask the teacher how much time your child should spend on homework.

- Set up a homework space such as a desk or the kitchen table. Be sure that there is good light and it is away from noise and the phone.

- Keep supplies at hand including paper, lined and unlined; pencils and colored pencils; pencil sharpener; dictionary; ruler.

- Agree with your child on homework rules such as when and where it will be done and what will happen if it is not done. Be consistent.

- Try to set up homework time when someone is available to help your child. If you cannot help, perhaps an older sibling or another relative can.

- Consider keeping the TV off until all children have had one hour to study or read. If you are also studying or doing your "homework" it will help.

- Help your child make a homework calendar to mark test dates and when assignments are due. Review it together often.

- Be sure your child understands all homework assignments. If he has a problem, work one or two problems with him. Do not do the homework for your child.

- Try to be patient and not become frustrated. Homework can be trying for both of you and your child may not be always clear about what he is to do. Losing your temper will not help.

- Call your child's teacher if you or your child do not understand an assignment.

- Look over your child's homework each night. Be sure all work is ready to go to school the next day.

- Review returned homework with your child.

- Set a good example by reading and limiting YOUR TV viewing.

- Praise your child for a job well done. Praise your child often.

Adapted from materials created by Beth Bochser, Contra Costa County (CA) Library's Project Second Chance, for her Families for Literacy Tutor Manuals 925–927–3250

YOU AND YOUR CHILD'S SCHOOL

- Keep a school file on each child for tests, report cards, school rules, medical reports, and phone numbers.

- Write important dates on your calendar: open house, field trips, class play.

- Write down the school phone number and carry it with you at all times. You may need to call the school if something unexpected comes up.

- Get to know the teacher. Attend open house, parent-teacher conferences, school events, and back to school nights.

- Call or write the teacher as soon as a problem comes up. Do not wait until your child falls too far behind.

- Do not be intimidated by the school and/or the teacher even through *your* school experience may not have been very positive. School staff really do want your child to succeed and your show of interest and concern will let them know that you support your child and want to help.

- Discuss school rules with your child and show your child that you support him/her.

- Send your child to school everyday, well-rested and well-fed.

- If your child misses a day of school, send a written note to the teacher explaining why he was out: sick, doctor appointment, family emergency. Do not you keep your child out of school unless it is necessary.

- Talk to your child about school. Spend the first 20 minutes after school or after you get home from work talking to your child about friends, recess, lunch, his/her teacher, math, etc.

- Consider volunteering at your child's school. Even if your literacy skills are not high, there are many things you can do to help at school.

Adapted from materials created by Beth Bochser, Contra Costa County (CA) Library's Project Second Chance, for her Families for Literacy Tutor Manuals
925–927–3250

OH NO! I'VE GOT A TEST!

- Children should be told to take tests seriously and do their best; however, they should not be afraid of them.

- Your child should write down everything that the teacher says about the test when it is announced. Then he/she will know how and what to study.

- Mark test dates on a calendar. Start studying well before the test using notes and texts.

- Parents can help by asking practice questions from the textbooks.

On the day of the test your child should

- Get normal rest or sleep the night before.

- Read or listen carefully to the directions. Ask the teacher to repeat anything that is unclear.

- If possible, look over the entire test before beginning and see how long it is.

- Watch the time and do not spend too long on any one problem. Mark difficult problems and go back to them if there is time.

- If there is time, go back and check for careless mistakes and unanswered problems.

When the test is returned

Review it with your child.
Praise him for strengths.
Help the child learn from mistakes.

Created by Beth Bochser, Contra Costa County (CA) Library's Project Second Chance, for her Families for Literacy Tutor Manuals 925–927–3250

APPENDIX G

Bibliography of Children's Books for Family Literacy

APPENDIX G
ANNOTATED BIBLIOGRAPHY OF CHILDREN'S BOOKS FOR FAMILY LITERACY

This bibliography was initiated by Robin Levy and Jane Curtis and expanded through contributions from Families For Literacy Coordinators in California Public Libraries.

TITLE	ISBN	AUTHOR	CHILD AGE	ADULT READING LEVEL	CONTENT
1,2,3 to the Zoo	039921970	Carle, E.	0-6	Beginning	practice with colors, numbers, and animals
A First Discovery Book-Flowers	059463837	Scholastic	3-9	Intermediate	children peek under petals to see what's inside
Abuela's Weave	1880000008	Castañeda, O.	6-10	Intermediate	Guatemalan grandmother & grandaughter work together
Adventures of Sparrowby	0689810717	Pinkey, B	7-12	Beginning	wordless picture book for older children
All the Magic in the World	0525450920	Hartmann, W.	4-8	Beginning-Intermediate	Black girl, imagination & self-esteem
Alphabet Tale, The	0688127029	Garten, J.	1-4	Beginning	ABC guessing, rhyming, animals game
Amazing Animal Facts	0679850856	Maynard, C.	6-12	Intermediate	photos, informational
Amazing Book of Shapes	156458514X	Sharman, L.	4-9	Intermediate	patterns, cut-out activities, spatial relations
Amazing Grace	0803710402	Hoffman, M.	4-9	Intermediate	Black girl, self-esteem, imagination
Andy's Pirate Ship	0805031545	Dupasquier, P.	5-10	Beginning-Intermediate	spot the difference, memory, pictures are busy
Angela's Wings	0374303312	Noves, E.	4-8	Beginning	Latino girl finds special self despite peers
Arthur's TV Trouble	0316109193	Brown, M.	3-8	Beginning-Intermediate	using TV positively
At the Beach	0805027688	Lee, H.	4-8	Beginning-Intermediate	mom & boy compare Chinese characters to objects
At The Library	0590728318	Loomis, C.	3-6	Beginning	visit to the library
Baby Just Like Me, A	1564586685	Winter, S.	3-7	Beginning-Intermediate	girl compares self with baby sibling
Baby Says	0688074235	Steptoe, J.	3-7	Beginning	Black older brother & baby, single words
Baby, The	0694005770	Greenfield, E.	3 mos-2	Beginning	Black family plays with baby, board book
Baby's Book of Nature	0789400030	Priddy, R.	0-4	Beginning	single words, counting, naming
Baseball Saved Us	1880000016	Mochizuki, K.	8-12	Intermediate-Advanced	Japanese internment camp; self-esteem; determination
Benny's Pennies	0385416024	Brisson, P.	3-6	Beginning	money, sharing, simple counting
Big Fat Hen	0152928693	Baker,K	3-6	Beginning	counting, concept book

TITLE	ISBN	AUTHOR	CHILD AGE	ADULT READING LEVEL	CONTENT
Big Machines	069400622X	Barton, B	2-5	Beginning	single word name for big machines/board book
Big Owl, Little Towel	068811783X	Allen, H.	6 mos-3	Beginning	single words, rhymes & opposites/board book
Black Is Brown Is Tan	0060200839	Adolph, A.	2-6	Beginning	identity
Born in the Gravy	0531086380	Cazet, D.	4-7	Intermediate	Latino father & daughter talk about kindergarten
Bouki Dances the Kokioko	0152000348	Walkstein, D.	7-9	Intermediate	comical Haitian Tale
Boundless Grace	0803717156	Hoffman, M.	7-11	Intermediate	African American girl reconnects with father in Africa
Bruno the Carpenter	0805045015	Klinting, L.	3-6	Beginning-Intermediate	beaver "carpenter" makes a tool box, tool vocab.
Brush Your Teeth Please	0895774747	McGuire, L.	3-5	Beginning	animal pop-up manipulative, interactive
Bug In A Rug	0688122086	Cole, J.	0-5	Beginning	terrific beginning fun
Bury My Bones but Keep My Words: African Tales for Retelling	0140368892	Fairman, T.	7-14	Advanced	13 stories from all over Africa
Can You Guess?	0688111815	Miller, M.	2-6	Beginning	Q & A multiple choice photos of multi-ethnic children
Car, Eyewitness Book of	0679907432		9-12	Intermediate	photo history of cars
Cars! Cars! Cars!	059047572X	Maccaroni, G.	1-4	Beginning	different cars/different colors/rhyming
Castles	0590463772	Jeunesse, G.	4-9	Intermediate	transparent overlays, Middle Ages
Cat Kong	0152420371	Pilkey, D.	4-8	Beginning-Intermediate	funny King Kong parody w/photos
Cat's Cradle	1878257536	Johnson, A.	8-12	Intermediate-Advanced	directions to make string shapes, string included
Chato's Kitchen	0399226583	Soto, G.	8-12	Intermediate-Advanced	hip, Latin language & rhythm, cat & mouse
Cheyenne Again	0395703646	Bunting, E.	9-12	Intermediate	Indian boy taken to boarding school retains his heritage
Chicka Chicka ABC	067187893X	Martin, B.	4-6	Beginning	simple ABC story
Children's Illustrated Dictionary	1564586251	McIlwain, J.	5-9	Intermediate	colorful photos, inviting introduction to dictionary use
Chrysthemum	0688147321	Henkes, K.	5-9	Intermediate	friendships, first day of school

TITLE	ISBN	AUTHOR	CHILD AGE	ADULT READING LEVEL	CONTENT
City Dog	0395661382	Kuskin, K.	2-5	Beginning	city dog romps in country
Clean Your Room, Harvey Moon	0027255115	Cummings, P.	5-9	Beginning-Intermediate	black mother uses consistent limits with son
Colors	0590452363	DeBourgoing, P.	4-8	Beginning	transparent pages overlay, color mixing
Colors (Fit a Shape Series)	156138707X	Running Press	0-4	Beginning	puzzle book of colors
Con Mi Hermano/With My Brother	0689718551	Roe, E.	3-7	Beginning	positive sibling role model, Spanish/English
Corduroy	0670241334	Freeman, D.	3-7	Intermediate	Black girl finds imperfect bear but makes own
Country Far Away, A	0531083926	Gray, N.	5-8	Beginning	cross-cultural similarities, simple sentences
Daddy	0060209232	Caines, J.	4-7	Beginning-Intermediate	Black dad visiting with daughter on weekend
Dancing	0531094669	Cazet, D.	3-7	Beginning	white dad reassures son after baby sibling is born
Day's Work, A	0395673216	Bunting, E.	9-12	Intermediate	Hispanic boy & grandfather, ethics
Dinosaur Stump	0525455914	Stickland, P.	3-8	Intermediate	lots of great dinosaurs
Dinosaur's Divorce	0316112488	Brown, L. & M.	5-11	Beginning-Intermediate	wide range of issues using dinosaur characters
Dinosaurs, Eyewitness Book of	0394822536		9-12	Intermediate	photo history of dinosaurs
Do I Have a Daddy?	093093444X	Lindsay, J.	3-8	Beginning	single mom tells son about his dad
Do Like Kyla	0531058522	Johnson, A.	3-8	Beginning	Black girl imitates older sister, good feelings
Doggies	0671493183	Boynton, S.	18 mos-3	Beginning	counting, series of sounds, board book
Dogzilla	0152239456	Pilkey, D.	4-8	Beginning-Intermediate	funny Godzilla parody w/photos
Dress I'll Wear to the Party, The	0688142613	Neitzel, S.	3-7	Beginning	rhyming, repetition, rebus (photos instead of words)
Edward the Emu	0207170517	Knowles, S.	4-7	Intermediate	comical look at one's self-esteem
Everyone Poops	0916291456	Gomi, T.	18 mos-4	Beginning	toilet training from animal perspective
Family That Fights, A	0807522481	Bernstein, S.	7-12	Intermediate	white boy's point of view, lots of text, guidelines

TITLE	ISBN	AUTHOR	CHILD AGE	ADULT READING LEVEL	CONTENT
Feast for 10	0395620376	Falwell, C.	3-6	Beginning	Black family, food, counting
Fiesta	0688143318	Guy, G.	3-6	Beginning	bilingual counting book
Fly Away Home	0395559626	Bunting, E.	5-10	Intermediate	homeless white father & son live in airport
Fox Got my Sox	0525449914	Offen, H.	18 mos-4	Beginning	body movements to go with rhymes
Freight Train	0688149006	Crews, D.	1-5	Beginning	Colors, train
Frog and Toad Together	006023959X	Lobel, A.	5-9	Beginning	short stories, humorous
Frog Goes to Dinner	0803733860	Mayer, M.	4-9	Wordless	pet frog makes mischief at restaurant
From 1 to 100	0525447644	Sloat, T.	3-7	Wordless	counting & finding images
Gathering the Sun	0688139043	Ada, A.	6-9	Intermediate-Advanced	bilingual alphabetical poems
Gathering the Sun: An Alphabet Book	0688139035	Ada, A. F.	3-9	Intermediate	beautiful illustrations on the fields and people working them
Girl Who Wore Snakes, The	0531054918	Johnson, A.	5-10	Beginning	Black girl finds place in family heritage
Giving	156402556X	Hughes, S.	2-7	Beginning	illustrates the concept of giving, simple sentences
Go Away, Big Green Monster	0316236535	Emberly, E.	4-7	Beginning	Halloween, create your own monster
Good Night, Gorilla	0399224459	Rothman, P.	2-7	Beginning-Intermediate	stimulates storytelling
Goodnight Moon	0694003611	Brown, M.	18 mos-3	Beginning	repetition, rhyme, noticing changes, board book
Gramma's Walk	0688114814	Hines, A.	5-9	Intermediate	white boy & grandma in wheel-chair; imagination
Grandfather and I	0688125344	Buckley, H.	3-5	Beginning	Black grandfather's special relationship w/grandson
Grandfather Tang's Story	051757487X	Tompert, A	10-13	Advanced	grandfather tells story with tangrams
Grandfather's Journey	0395570352	Say, A.	5-9	Intermediate-Advanced	Asian-American cross-cultural identity; historical
Grandma	155379674	Bailey, D.	1-3	Beginning	photos, multi-ethnic, board book
Grandmother's Nursery Rhymes	0805025553	Jaramillo, N.	3-7	Beginning	Spanish/English, short, simple verses
Grandpa	1550379666	Bailey, D.	1-3	Beginning	photos, multi-ethnic, board book

TITLE	ISBN	AUTHOR	CHILD AGE	ADULT READING LEVEL	CONTENT
Grandpa Toad's Secrets	0399226109	Kasza, K.	5-9	Beginning-Intermediate	wisdom passes to grandson who uses it to save grandpa
Guess How Much I Love You	1564024733	McBratney, S.	2-6	Intermediate	father bunny loves child even more than child loves father
Handmade Alphabet, The	0803709749	Rankin, L.	2-8	Beginning	beautifully illustrated sign alphabet
Harlem	0590543407	Myers, W.	10-adult	Advanced	wonderful, rich book, great illustrations
Hats, Hats, Hats	0688063381	Morris, Ann	3-9	Beginning	multicultural look via photos of hats around world
Hats Off To Hair	0881068683	Kroll, V.	3-7	Intermediate	multicultural/different hair
Hello! Good-bye!	0688143342	Aliki	4-8	Intermediate	different hellos/good-byes/cultural differences
Henry's Baby	1564581969	Hoffman, M.	7-11	Intermediate	big brother cares for baby & gains peer acceptance
Hey, I'm Reading	0679956441	Miles, Betty	3-6	Beginning	reading readiness, story, collection
Hi!	0399219641	Scott, A.	3-5	Beginning	Latino child greets patrons in post office
How a House is Built	0823412326	Gibbons, G.	4-8	Beginning	simple pictures; vocab about building materials
How Smudge Came	0802775225	Gregory, N.	6-11	Advanced	Down syndrome woman's determination to keep puppy
How to Lose All Your Friends	0670849065	Carlson, N.	4-9	Beginning	humorous look at unacceptable social behavior
I Can't Talk About It	0880701498	Sanford, D.	6-12	Beginning-Intermediate	girl faces sexual abuse, healing, trust
I Hate English	0590423053	Levine, E.	7-11	Intermediate-Advanced	Chinese girl learns English but loves her first language
I Like Books	0394841867	Browne, A.	1-5	Beginning	monkey characters, all kinds of books
I Like Me	0670820628	Carlson, N.	3-7	Beginning	girl pig, self-esteem, simple sentences
I Promise I'll Find You	1895565405	Ward, H.	3-8	Beginning	rhyming verse, love, commitment, reassurance
I Spy Mystery	0590462946	Marzollo, J.	5-10	Beginning	find objects in photos, rhyming
I Took My Frog to the Library	014050916X	Kimmel, E.	3-7	Beginning	girl bring different animals into library

TITLE	ISBN	AUTHOR	CHILD AGE	ADULT READING LEVEL	CONTENT
I Touch	0152588493	Isadora, R.	1-4	Beginning	toddler touches different things
I Went Walking	0152007717	Williams, S.	1-4	Beginning	identify colors and animals
I Wish I Had a Father	0807535222	Simon, N.	4-9	Beginning-Intermediate	white boy never sees dad, hates Father's Day
I Wish I Was Sick Too!	068809354X	Brandenberg	3-5	Beginning	child envies attention given to sick brother
If...	0892363215	Perry, S.	4-8	Beginning	beautiful illustrations lead reader to imagine if...
In and Out	0671866303	Carter, D.	0-3	Beginning	learning prepositions/pop-up board book
In & Out The Window	0916147460	Bandel, J.	3-6	Intermediate-Advanced	children's poetry
Is Your Mama a Llama?	0590413872	Guarino, D.	2-5	Beginning	rhyming animal guessing game
It Looked Like Spilt Milk	069400491X	Shaw, C.	2-4	Beginning	board book of shapes, repetition
It's Perfectly Normal	1564021998	Harris, R.	10-15	Intermediate	candid developmental sex info, great drawings
It's Raining Laughter	0803720033	Grimes, N.	3-8	Intermediate	poems about children playing
Jamaica Tag-Along	0395496020	Havill, J.	4-9	Beginning-Intermediate	Black girl feels left-out by older brother
Jobs for Kids	068809323X	Barkin & James	6-12	Intermediate-Advanced	promote work ethic for ages 6-12
John Patrick Norman McHennessy	0517568055	Burningham, J.	5-9	Beginning-Intermediate	school, authority, punishment, truth
Jonathan and His Mommy	0316798703	Smalls-Hector, I.	3-7	Beginning-Intermediate	Black boy & mom walk in different ways together
Julius, the Baby of the World	0688089437	Henkes, K.	3-8	Beginning-Intermediate	girl mouse feels upstaged by baby brother
King of the Playground	0689315589	Naylor, P.	5-9	Intermediate	white father & son solve bully problem
Koala Lou	0152005021	Fox, M.	7-10	Intermediate	self-esteem & family support
Laughing Tomatoes	0892391391	Risuenos, J.	3-7	Intermediate	bilingual poems about spring
Leo the Late Bloomer	0878070427	Kraus, R.	3-7	Beginning	developmental timing, self-esteem
Let's Pretend	0694005916	Moore, D. & C.	2-4	Beginning	Black girl imitates adults, board book
Life is Fun	0670842060	Carlson, N.	4-7	Beginning	self-esteem & moral values, simple sentences

TITLE	ISBN	AUTHOR	CHILD AGE	ADULT READING LEVEL	CONTENT
Little Monsters	0843129646	Pienkowski, J.	2-5	Beginning	tiny, pop-up, rhyme, interactive
Little Pigeon Toad	0671666592	Gwynne, F.	7-10	Beginning	illustrated puns & word plays
Long Journey Home: Stories from Black History	0140389814	Lester, J.	7-14	Intermediate-Advanced	stories of Black history retold by well-known authors
Look Again! Second Ultimate . . .	0803709587	Wood, A.	7-12	Wordless	complex animal habitats, beautiful illustrations
Look! The Ultimate . . .	0803709250	Wood, A.	7-12	Wordless	complex animal habitats, beautiful illustrations
Lots of Moms	0803718918	Rotner & Kelly	2-5	Beginning	multi-ethnic photos, simple text
Loving	0688145523	Morris, A.	3-7	Beginning	models what it means to be a parent; multicultural
Lunch with Cat and Dog	0916119920	Williams, R.L.	3-7	Intermediate	cat and dog divide lunch into fractions
Malcom X: By Any Means Necessary	059066221X	Myers, W.	9-12	Advanced	life of Civil Rights leader with photos
Mama, Do You Love Me?	087701759X	Joose, B.	3-7	Beginning	Eskimo imagery, reassurance, Q & A, repetition
Margaret and Margarita	0688122396	Reisner, L.	4-8	Beginning	girls & moms, bilingual Spanish/English, friendship
Max and Ruby's Greek Myths	0803715242	Wells, R.	3-8	Beginning-Intermediate	Pandora story, limit-setting for younger brother
Max's Chocolate Chicken	0803705859	Wells, R.	3-7	Beginning	Easter egg hunt & issues of sibling age advantages
Max's Dragon Shirt	0803709447	Wells, R.	3-7	Beginning	rabbit Ruby takes brother Max clothes shopping
Me First	0395587069	Lester, H.	6-9	Intermediate	pig boy & appropriate social behavior
Meet Danitra Brown	0688154719	Grimes, N.	5-10	Intermediate	poems in first person. Point of view of Black Girl
Miss Malarkey Doesn't Live in Room 10	0802774989	Finchler, J.	5-8	Intermediate	boy finds teacher has life outside of classroom
Miss Tizzy	0671775901	Gray, L.	7-10	Intermediate-Advanced	dealing with loss
Mom Goes to Work	0590462881	Gleeson, L.	3-8	Beginning	multi-ethnic moms do different work, simple text
More More More	0688091733	Williams, V.	1-4	Beginning	multi-ethnic families play with toddlers; sequencing

TITLE	ISBN	AUTHOR	CHILD AGE	ADULT READING LEVEL	CONTENT
Mother for Choco, A	0399218416	Kasza, K.	3-8	Beginning	baby bird finds a mother in a bear who loves it truly
Mouse TV	0531068560	Novak, M.	3-8	Beginning	mouse family uses imagination without tv
Moving Day	0688139485	Kalan, R.	3-6	Beginning	dealing with the changes in moving
My Best Shoes	0688117570	Burton, M.	3-5	Beginning	multicultural & individual differences
My Dad	0689506201	Daly, N.	8-12	Intermediate	children's perspective of alcoholic father
My Day/Mi Día	0316234508	Emberly, R.	3-8	Beginning	object-naming, bilingual Spanish/English
My First Book of Proverbs	0892391340	Gonzalez, R.	3-6	Intermediate	bilingual proverbs, great pictures
My First Look at Numbers	0679805338	McKay	2-5	Beginning	color photos, object identification
My First Look at Sizes	067980532X	McKay	3-7	Beginning	size identification & comparison
My First Number Book	1879431734	Heinst, M.	3-8	Beginning	math concepts of pairs, sets, addition, subtraction
My First Science Book	0679805834	Wilkes, A.	5-10	Intermediate	simple experiments, visual directions
My Mama Needs Me	0688061707	Walter, M.	4-8	Beginning-Intermediate	Black boy wants to help mom with new baby
My Mom	1550371630	Bailey, D.	1-3	Beginning	simple, multi-ethnic pictures, board book
My Very First Mother Goose	1564026205	Opie, I.	3-7	Intermediate	traditional Mother Goose
Night Rabbits	0525453350	Wellington, M.	3-5	Beginning	rabbits have fun at night
Now I'm Big	0688140785	Miller, M.	2-5	Beginning	multi-ethnic children remember being babies
Numbers	0671769081	Tucker, S.	6 mos-2	Beginning	small board book, single words
Octopus Hug	1563970341	Pringle, L.	5-9	Intermediate	Black father & children rough-house
Officer Buckle and Gloria	0399226168	Rathmann, P.	3-9	Intermediate	working together is better
Old MacDonald	0531094936	Souhami, J.	3-6	Beginning-Intermediate	funny twist on familiar song
On Mother's Lap	0395589207	Scott, A.	2-4	Beginning	Eskimo toddler & baby share mother
One Frog Too Many	0803748388	Mayer, M.	4-9	Wordless	sibling rivalry between frogs

TITLE	ISBN	AUTHOR	CHILD AGE	ADULT READING LEVEL	CONTENT
One More River to Cross: 12 Stories	0590428977	Haskins, J.	9-12	Intermediate-Advanced	short accounts of black heroes
One More Time	0688065864	Baum, L.	3-5	Beginning	white dad with toddler for weekend visit; simple
One Yellow Lion	0803710992	Van Fleet, M.	2-7	Beginning	fold-out counting, colors, visual memory
Our Granny	0395883954	Wild, M.	3-8	Beginning	dispels myths about grandmothers; diversity
Out of the Ocean	0152588493	Frasier, D.	2-10	Intermediate	family walking on beach finds objects from ocean
Owl Babies	1564021017	Waddell, M.	3-7	Beginning	baby owls miss mom but she always comes back
Owl Eyes	0688124739	Gates, F.	6-10	Beginning-Intermediate	Native American legend
Pablo's Tree	0027674010	Mora, P.	4-8	Beginning-Intermediate	Latino boy & grandpa, tradition, birthday
Pain and the Great One, The	0027111008	Blume, J.	4-9	Intermediate	white brother & sister think parents love other best
Panda, Panda	0688065643	Hoban, T.	1-3	Beginning	identifying verbs, single words, board book
Papa and Me	0876148437	Miyamoto, T.	3-8	Beginning-Intermediate	bears, father & son share memories
Paperboy, The	0531095061	Pilkey, D.	4-7	Intermediate	gentle story about a paper boy & a dog
Pearl Moskowitz's Last Stand	0688107532	Levine, A.	6-11	Intermediate-Advanced	changing neighborhoods
Peter's Chair	0064430405	Keats, E. J.	3-5	Beginning	a new baby
Phone Book, The	084312970	Pienkowski, J.	3-6	Beginning	pop-up, push button, rhyme, interactive
Pig Pig Grows Up	0140547797	McPhail, D.	2-8	Intermediate	baby pig learns growing up is not so bad
Pigs Aplenty, Pigs Galore	0140553134	McPhail, D.	2-5	Beginning	simple rhymes, fun book about pigs visiting
Pigsty	0590698206	Teague, M.	3-8	Intermediate	visit from messy pigs convinces child to clean room
Read to Your Bunny	0590302841	Wells, R.	0-4	Beginning	parents read with children 20 minutes each day

TITLE	ISBN	AUTHOR	CHILD AGE	ADULT READING LEVEL	CONTENT
Rebels Against Slavery	0590457365	McKissack, P.	7-14	Advanced	American slave revolts, including one by Cinque
Rib Ticklers	0688125190	Sloat, T.	10-13	Intermediate-Advanced	jokes with a theme, plays on words
Rough Face Girl, The	0399218599	Miller, M.	8-12	Intermediate	American Indian Cinderella story/ what is true beauty
See How I Grow	156458464X	Wilkes, A.	2-5	Beginning	child development, birth to three yrs
Shapes (Fit a Shape Series)	1561387096	Running Press	0-4	Beginning	match a shape board book
Sheila Rae, the Brave	0688071554	Henkes, K.	4-9	Beginning-Intermediate	girl mouse admires older sister & helps her
Shortcut	068806437X	Crews, D.	5-8	Beginning	Black rural, truth & consequences
Shy Charles	0803705646	Wells, R.	5-8	Beginning	individual differences, parental expectations; rabbits
Smoky Night	0152699546	Bunting, E.	4-9	Intermediate	LA riots, interracial relationships
Snoozers	0689817746	Boynton, S.	1-5	Beginning	board book, great table of contents
Snow	0374370923	Shulevitz, U.	2-8	Beginning	visual, joyful look at snow, great illustrations
So Much	1564023443	Cooke, T.	3-8	Beginning-Intermediate	Black family, rhyme, sequencing, vernacular
Socrates	081181047X	Bogaerts, R. & G.	3-7	Intermediate	dog finds friendship and sharing important
Something Must Be Wrong	0880704691	Sanford, D.	6-12	Intermediate	boy faces sexual abuse, healing, trust
Sports, Eyewitness Book of	0394896165	Hammond, T.	8-12	Intermediate-Advanced	visual history of various sports
Squids Will Be Squids	067088135X	Scieozka, J.	9-15	Intermediate	very funny play on fables
Stanley and Rhoda	014054707X	Wells, R.	3-7	Beginning	three sibling stories, brother & sister rabbits
Stitching Stars: Story Quilts of Harriet Powers (African-American Artists and Artisans)	068981707X	Lyons, M.	8-14	Intermediate-Advanced	Women's quilts are African American folk art/treasures
Storm in the Night	0060259124	Stolz, M.	6-11	Intermediate-Advanced	Black grandfather & grandson deal with fear
Suddenly	0152016446	McNaughty, C.	4-8	Beginning-Intermediate	pig avoids incompetent wolf, making predictions
Ten, Nine, Eight	0688009069	Bang, M.	1-3	Beginning	Black girl's bedtime, rhyming, counting

TITLE	ISBN	AUTHOR	CHILD AGE	ADULT READING LEVEL	CONTENT
The Cheerios Play Book	0689822804	Wade, L.	2-5	Beginning	fun with Cheerios and eye-hand coordination
The Grouchy Ladybug	0064434508	Carle, E.	3-5	Intermediate	ladybug tries to pick arguments; colors and time
The Leaving Morning	053107077	Johnson, A.	3-8	Intermediate	family leaving home
There's a Nightmare in My Closet	0803786824	Mayer, M.	2-6	Beginning	making friends with nightmares
Three Science Flip Books	0316234567	Emberly, E.	5-9	Wordless	flip pages to make life cycles of six animals & plants
Too Far Away to Touch	0395689686	Newman, L.	5-9	Intermediate	death of uncle from AIDS, sensitive handling
Too Much Talk	0763603982	Medearis, A.	4-8	Intermediate	West African folktale adaptation about nonhuman things that suddenly can talk (a yam, a fish)
Tools	0694006238	Barton, B.	2-5	Beginning	one-word ID/board book
Tortillas & Lullabies/Tortillas y Concioncioncitas	0688146287	Ruser, L.	2-6	Beginning	family love/bilingual Spanish-English
Two Eyes, a Nose and a Mouth	0590482475	Intrater, R.	2-8	Beginning	photos, simple rhyming text, celebrate diversity
Two Greedy Bears	002736450X	Ginsburg, M.	3-7	Beginning	competition, animal fable
Uncle Ted's Barbershop	0689819317	Mitchell, M.	5-10	Intermediate	uncle makes sacrifices to care for someone
Uno, Dos, Tres; One, Two, Three	0395672945	Mora, P.	2-8	Beginning	bilingual, great pictures, numbers
Visual Dictionary of Cars, The	1564580075	Brown, Deni	9-12	Intermediate	photo history of cars
Visual Dictionary of Everyday Things (Eyewitness Visual Dictionaries)	1879431173	Brown, Deni	5-10	Intermediate	common objects taken apart & labeled
Way Mothers Are, The	0807586919	Schlein, M.	3-8	Beginning	cat mom defines love for kitten son
Wednesday Surprise, The	0395547768	Bunting, E.	5-10	Intermediate	grandaughter teaches grand-mother to read
What a Wonderful World	0689800878	Weiss & Thiele	4-8	Beginning	kids create puppet show to Louis Armstrong song
What Am I Doing in a Stepfamily	0818405635	Berman, C. G.	4-10	Intermediate	adjusting to a stepfamily, candid Q & A
What Daddies Do Best/Mommies	0689805772	Numeroff, L.	4-8	Beginning	what daddies do best/flip book to what mommies do best

TITLE	ISBN	AUTHOR	CHILD AGE	ADULT READING LEVEL	CONTENT
What's Missing?	0317043498	Yektai, N.	2-5	Wordless	humorous, simple, spot-the-difference
Wheels (Fit a Shape Series)	0762402415	Running Press	0-4	Beginning	match a shape board book of wheels
When a Parent Doesn't Speak English	082391691X	Lakin, P.	9-12	Intermediate	immigrants' stories
When Jo Louis Won the Title	0395666147	Rochelle, B.	9-12	Intermediate	Black pride, gender, family history
When Mom Turned into a Monster	1575050137	Harrison, J.	5-9	Beginning-Intermediate	white mom tries to clean house while kids mess it up
Where's My Teddy?	1564020487	Alborough, J.	3-5	Beginning	size discrimination, rhyming
Which Way, Ben Bunny	0590622455	Smith, Mavis	3-5	Beginning	learning right & left
White Bead Ceremony	0933031920	Watkins, S.	9-12	Intermediate	Native American traditions brought into present day
Who Ate It?	1562948423	Gomi, T.	2-5	Beginning	find the image game, repetition
Who Hid It?	1562940112	Gomi, T.	2-5	Beginning	find the image game, repetition
Who's Counting	0688061311	Tafuri, Nancy	2-5	Beginning	counting, hide and seek
Who's in a Family?	1883672139	Skutch, R.	2-7	Beginning	multi-ethnic, socially diverse lifestyles
Why Am I Different?	0807590762	Simon, N.	4-9	Beginning-Intermediate	how children are different in daily life
Why Are We Getting a Divorce?	0517565277	Mayle, P.	7-12	Intermediate-Advanced	honest, humorous chronology of divorce, lots of text
Why Do You Love Me?	0688091563	Baynton, M.	3-6	Beginning	white dad & son talk about love
Wiley & the Hairy Man	068981142X	Bang, M.	4-8	Intermediate	adaptation of African American folk tale /scary
Wilfrid Gordon McDonald	0916291049	Fox, M.	4-8	Beginning	white boy's relationship with old people
Willie's Not the Hugging Kind	0060204168	Barrett, J.	6-9	Intermediate	Black boy develops own values against peer pressure
Willy the Wimp	0394826108	Browne, A.	7-11	Beginning	self-image, peer pressure, bullying
Wilma Unlimited	0152012672	Krull, K.	7-12	Intermediate	Wilma Rudolph overcomes polio to win gold medal
Work	0688148662	Morris, A.	3-7	Intermediate	families and children involved in work
Work Song	0152009809	Paulsen, R.	3-6	Beginning	beautiful illustrations of various careers

TITLE	ISBN	AUTHOR	CHILD AGE	ADULT READING LEVEL	CONTENT
Yawn Goes On, The	0525450769	Ward, S.	2-5	Beginning	continuous hole in small board book
Yo! Yes!	0531054691	Raschke, C.	4-8	Beginning	Black boy & white boy connect with just a few words
You & Me: Poems of Friendship	0531300455	Mavor, S.	3-6	Beginning	great friendship poems
You're My Nikki	0803711298	Eisenberg, P.	3-7	Intermediate	Black girl & mom, reassurance & specialness
Zoo Animals	0694006203	Barton, B.	2-5	Beginning	animals in the zoo/board book
Zoo Doings	0671865994	Zoological Society	2-5	Beginning	single action words, great pictures, board book
Zoom	0670858048	Banyai, I.	7-12	Wordless	one-world, pictures within pictures, perspective

APPENDIX H

Family Literacy Parent Survey

APPENDIX H
FAMILY LITERACY
PARENT SURVEY

**INSTRUCTIONS
FOR
FAMILIES FOR LITERACY PARENT SURVEY**

The Families For Literacy Parent Survey (FFLPS) is to be used as a tool for:

- Tracking of progress by individual families and their tutors
- Tracking of progress by individual library programs as an evaluation of their own programs and the effectiveness of their training
- Evaluating and assessing progress of all FFL families in the state in order to provide state-wide information for funding and accountability purposes.

How to use:

1. Each FFL parent/primary caregiver should complete a Pre-Families For Literacy Parent Survey upon **entry into the program**. These can be completed with help from local staff or the tutor of the adult learner. If a family was in your program *last* year, their *Post* Survey July 97/98 will be used as their *Pre* for 98/99.

2. Every FFL family should complete a Post FFLPS in June 1999 **or upon leaving** the program, whichever comes first. These can be completed with help from local staff or the adult's tutor.

3. Please see that responses are given for questions 1–11 by **all** FFL families. It may be helpful to use more than one form if the family includes more than one child and the parent has difficulty responding with a single answer for all children.

4. If English is not the parent's first language, then questions 12–13 should be completed.

5. If the family includes one or more children of kindergarten age or older, then the parent needs to respond to the second set of questions 14–17.

6. All **Pre/Post FFLPS** forms should be duplicated and the *originals mailed to the California State Library with your FINAL Report.* **Send all Pre-FFLPS forms, even if you were unable to get a Post-FFLPS.** Make every effort to have a Post FFLPS even if the family leaves before they have been in your program for 6 months.

7. Confidentiality is guaranteed. Individual families will be assigned a code number and will not be identified by name in any research or results reported.

THANK YOU FOR YOUR ATTENTION TO THIS IMPORTANT SURVEY!!

FY 1998/99

FAMILIES FOR LITERACY PARENT SURVEY
FOR CALIFORNIA LIBRARY PROGRAMS

Name of Library _____ Pre ❏ or Post ❏ Survey *(check one)*

Date of Learner's Entry _____ Date of Survey _____

Learner's Name _____

Child(ren)'s Birth Date(s) _____

Tutor's Name _____

FFL Tutors,
Please fill out the survey with your learner and then return it to the literacy office. Complete the pre-survey when you are matched with your adult learner. Complete the post-survey if your learner leaves the program, or in June 1999. If one survey does not work for all of your learner's children then fill out a separate survey for each child.

Please ✓ one box for each question.	Never	1–2 times a year	1–2 times a month	1 time a week	2–3 times a week	everyday
1. How often does your child ask you to read books to him?	❏	❏	❏	❏	❏	❏
2. How often does your child look at books by himself?	❏	❏	❏	❏	❏	❏
3. How often do you share books or magazines with your child? When? _____	❏	❏	❏	❏	❏	❏
4. How often do you add to your child's book collection?	❏	❏	❏	❏	❏	❏
5. How often does your child use art supplies? (paper, crayons, scissors, chalk)	❏	❏	❏	❏	❏	❏

	Never	1–2 times a year	1–2 times a month	1 time a week	2–3 times a week	everyday
6. How often does your child see that you read and write?	❑	❑	❑	❑	❑	❑
7. How often do you borrow library books with your child?	❑	❑	❑	❑	❑	❑
8. How often do you go to storytimes with your child?	❑	❑	❑	❑	❑	❑
9. How often do you sing, recite rhymes and/or play games with your child?	❑	❑	❑	❑	❑	❑
10. How often do you tell stories to your child?	❑	❑	❑	❑	❑	❑

11. When sharing a book with your child, does the book hold his attention for:
(Choose only *one*)

Five minutes or less? ❑   Ten to fifteen minutes? ❑

Fifteen to twenty minutes? ❑   Thirty minutes or more? ❑

If English is _not_ your first language, how often do you...

	Never	1–2 times a year	1–2 times a month	1 time a week	2–3 times a week	everyday
12. ... read to your child in *your* first language?	❑	❑	❑	❑	❑	❑
13. ... read to your child in English?	❑	❑	❑	❑	❑	❑

If you have a child(ren) in kindergarten or older, then fill out this section also:

Name(s) & grade(s) of child(ren) in school _____

	Never	1–2 times a year	1–2 times a month	1 time a week	2–3 times a week	everyday
Please ✓ one box for each question.						
14. How often do you go to parent meetings or other school activities?	❏	❏	❏	❏	❏	❏
15. How often do you write notes to or call your child's teacher?	❏	❏	❏	❏	❏	❏
16. How often do you help your child with homework?	❏	❏	❏	❏	❏	❏
17. How often does your child have a place, a special time, and the materials to do homework?	❏	❏	❏	❏	❏	❏

revised 9/98

APPENDIX I

Bibliography of Selected Family Literacy Publications

APPENDIX I
BIBLIOGRAPHY OF
USEFUL FAMILY
LITERACY PUBLICATIONS

(Developed by Dr. Carole Talan for the Families for Literacy Programs)

Anderson, Richard, E. Hiebert, J. Scott, and I. Wilkinson, *Becoming a Nation of Readers: The Report of the Commission on Reading.* Urbana: Center for the Study of Reading, University of Illinois, 1985.

de Avila, Marcia, Donna Lednicky, and Katy Pruitt. "Family Literacy: Holistic Approaches to Family Literacy Facilitate Learning of At-Risk Families." *Adult Learning* (September/October 1993): 15–16+.

Berlin, Gordon, and Andrew Sum. *Toward a More Perfect Union: Basic Skills, Poor Families, and Our Economic Future.* New York: Ford Foundation, 1988.

Blum, Deborah. "Fetuses fond of Dr. Seuss, Study Finds." *The Sacramento Bee*, Sunday, October 8, 1989, A17.

Barbara Bush Foundation for Family Literacy. *First Teachers.* Washington, D.C.: Barbara Bush Foundation, 1989.

Beyond Rhetoric: A New American Agenda for Children and Families: Summary. Washington, D.C.: National Commission on Children, 1991.

Binkley, Marilyn R. *Becoming a Nation of Readers: What Parents Can Do.* Champaign, Ill.: D.C. Heath, March 1988.

Edelman, Peter, and Beryl A. Radin. *Serving Children and Families Effectively: How the Past Can Help the Future.* Washington, D.C.: Education and Human Services Consortium, 1992.

Handel, Ruth, and Ellen Goldsmith. "Children's Literature and Adult Literacy: Empowerment through Intergenerational Learning." *Lifelong Learning* (1989): 24–27.

———. *Family Reading: An Intergenerational Approach to Literacy.* Syracuse, N.Y.: New Reader's Press, 1990.

Hauser, Jill Frankel. *Learning and Loving to Read.* Redding, Calif.: Learning Excellence Press, 1990.

Heath, Shirley Brice, "What No Bedtime Story Means: Narrative Skills at Home and School." *Language in Society* (1982): 11, 49–76.

Hills, T.W. "Finding What Is of Value in Programs for Young Children and Their Families." *Continuing Issues in Early Childhood Education.* S. Bredekamp and t. Rosegrant (Eds.), Upper Saddle River, N.J.: Prentice-Hall, 1997, 2nd ed., 293–313.

Johnson, Debra Wilcox, and Leslie Edmonds. *Family Literacy Library Programs: Models of Service.* Des Moines, Ia.: State Library of Iowa, 1990.

Literacy Volunteers of America. *How to Start a Family Literacy Project.* Syracuse, N.Y.: Literacy Volunteers of America, 1991.

McGee, Lea M., and Donald J. Richgels. *Literacy's Beginnings: Supporting Young Readers And Writers.* Boston: Allyn and Bacon, 1990.

McIvor, M. Conlon, ed. *Family Literacy in Action: A Survey of Successful Programs.* Syracuse, N.Y.: New Readers Press, 1990.

Monsour, Margaret, and Carole Talan. *Library-Based Family Literacy Projects.* Chicago. American Library Association, 1992.

Nash, Andrea. *English Family Literacy: An Annotated Bibliography.* Boston: English Family Literacy Project, University of Massachusetts, 1987.

National Center for Family Literacy. *A Guide to Funding Sources for Family Literacy.* Louisville, Ky.: National Center for Family Literacy, 1991.

Nickse, Ruth S. "Family Literacy Programs: Ideas for Action." *Adult Learning* (February 1990): 9–13+.

———. *Family and Intergenerational Literacy Programs: An Update of "The Noises of Literacy."* Columbus, Ohio: ERIC Clearinghouse on Adult, Career, and Vocational Education. Ohio State University, 1990.

Nickse, Ruth S., A. Speicher, and P. Bucheck. "An Inter-generational Literacy Project: A Family Intervention/ Prevention Model." *Journal of Reading* 31 (1988): 634–642.

Lancaster, Alden. *An Introduction to Intergenerational Literacy.* Washington, D.C.: Wider Opportunities for Women, Inc., 1992.

Potts, Meta. *The Past, Present and Promise of Family Literacy. The Bookmark* 50, no. III (Spring, 1992): 236–238.

Quezada, Shelly, and Ruth Nickse. *Community Collaborations for Family Literacy Handbook.* New York: Neal-Schuman, 1993.

Rangel, Elizabeth. "A Primer on English Family Literacy Programs." *The Ladder* (January/February, 1991): 6–9.

Rasinski, Timothy, and Anthony Fredericks. "Sharing Literacy: Guiding Principles and Practices for Parent Involvement." *The Reading Teacher* (February 1988): 509–512.

Stief, E.A. *The Role of Parent Education in Achieving School Readiness.* Washington, D.C.: National Governors' Association.

Sticht, Tom. *Teach the Mother—Reach the Child, Intergenerational Literacy Action Research Project.* Washington, D.C.: Wider Opportunities for Women, 1991.

Sticht, Tom, and Barbara McDonald. *Making the Nation Smarter: The Intergenerational Transfer of Cognitive Ability.* University Park, Penn.: Institute for the Study of Adult Literacy, Pennsylvania State University (1989).

Snow, Catherine, M. Susan Burns, and Peg Griffin, eds. *Preventing Reading Difficulties in Young Children.* Washington, D.C.: National Research Council, 1998.

Strickland, Dorothy S., and Lesley Mandel Morrow, eds. *Emerging Literacy: Young Children Learn to Read and Write.* Newark: International Reading Association, 1989.

Talan, Carole. "Families for Literacy: Breaking the Cycle of Illiteracy." *California State Library Foundation Bulletin* (July 1989): 6–10.

———. "Family Literacy Makes ene: Families That Read Together Succeed." *The Bottom Line, A Financial Magazine for Librarians* (Winter/Spring 1994): 46–51.

————. "Family Literacy: Libraries Doing What Libraries Do Best." *Wilson Library Bulletin.* (November 1990): 30–32+.

————. "Real-Life Empowerment through Family-Centered Literacy." *American Libraries* (December 1998): 49–51.

Taylor, Denny. *From the Child's Point of View.* Portsmouth, N.H.: Heineman Educational Books, 1990.

————. *Family Literacy: Young Children Learning to Read and Write.* Portsmouth, N.H.: Heinemann Educational Books, 1983.

Taylor, Denny, and Catherine Dorsey-Gaines. *Growing Up Literate: Learning from Inner-City Families.* Portsmouth, N.H.: Heineman Educational Books, 1988.

Turner, Molly, and Nancy Kober. *From Thibodaux to Tucumcari: Family Literacy in Rural Libraries.* Washington, D.C.: Center for the Book, Library of Congress, 1997.

Weiss, Heather B., and Francine H. Jacobs, eds. *Evaluating Family Literacy Programs.* New York, N.Y.: Aldine de Gruyter, 1988.

White, Dorothy. *Books before Five.* Portsmouth, N.H.: Heinemann, 1984.

VIDEOS

Close to Home: Library-Based Family Literacy. (24 min). Bell Atlantic/ALA Family Literacy Project. Chicago: American Library Association, 1992.

Enrique's Story. (7.5 min). Sacramento: California State Library Foundation, 1994.

Families for Literacy. (15 min). Sacramento: California State Library Foundation, 1992.

LITTLE BEGINNINGS: Starting Your Child on a Lifetime of Learning. (18 min). Elk Grove Village, Ill.: World Book Educational Products, 1994.

A New Baby in My House. (30 min). Children's Television Workshop. New York: Random House Home Video, 1994.

INDEX